GOLF SAYINGS

wit & wisdom of a good walk spoiled

By Bradford G. Wheler

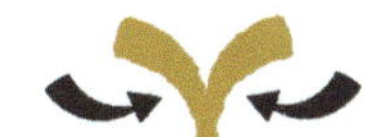

BookCollaborative.com
Cazenovia, NY 13035

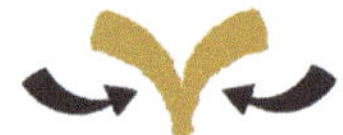

BookCollaborative.com
PO box 403
Cazenovia, NY 13035
BookCollaborative.com@gmail.com

ISBN-13 978-0-9822538-5-4

Library of Congress Control Number: 2013914257
Golf, Quotations, Art, Humor & Wit

PRINTED IN THE UNITED STATES OF AMERICA

Cover design by AuthorSupport.com
Interior design by Adina Cucicov, Flamingo Designs

US Retail Price $24.95

Table of Contents

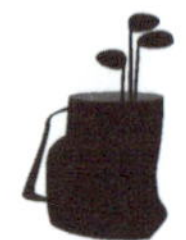

Introduction

I would like to thank everyone who participated in this project. In particular, I wanted to thank the artists and photographers who contributed their original works to this book.

It was exciting to check my email and find a wonderful range of new submissions from a wide variety of artists and photographers. The book features over 36 artists from 10 different countries. Many of the artists in this book are full time professional artists or photographers. Others love painting and photographing as a hobby. They exhibit a wonderful range of artistic styles. Many are avid golfers.

I established BookCollaborative.com to publish books based on the content provided by artists. The goal is to create a collaborative community to promote art in general. At the same time, artists have the opportunity to promote their own artwork in books. I also want it to be interesting and fun. For more information go to www.BookCollaborative.com.

In selecting images for GOLF SAYINGS, I tried to be inclusive. However, some artwork simply didn't fit the theme of this book. Other artwork did not make the cut due to various factors, such as missing the deadline, low image resolution, etc.

Printing color books with Lightening Source Inc's on demand system is about six times more expensive as printing black and white books. This factor limits the page count of a reasonably priced color book. It's my hope that as technology progresses, the price for color

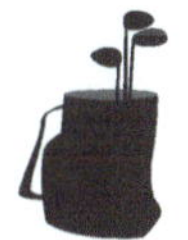

on demand printing will come down. This would allow greater flexibility in the size of color books as well as the number of pages.

This book would not have been possible without the help of many other individuals. They include; Adina Cucicov of Flamingo Design, who has done a beautiful job with the book's interior design. Nancy Kelner who turns my sloppy first drafts into a workable format. Brian Hoke of Bentley Hoke Consulting who helped with all things web related. Simon, and others from the Apple store One to One training team who patiently keep teaching me. I would like to thank my lovely wife Julie for her support on this project and everything else.

I'm sure this book includes errors and for those I apologize.

Most of all, I hope people enjoy *"GOLF SAYINGS; wit and wisdom of a good walk spoiled."*

Bradford G. Wheler
Cazenovia, NY
October 2013

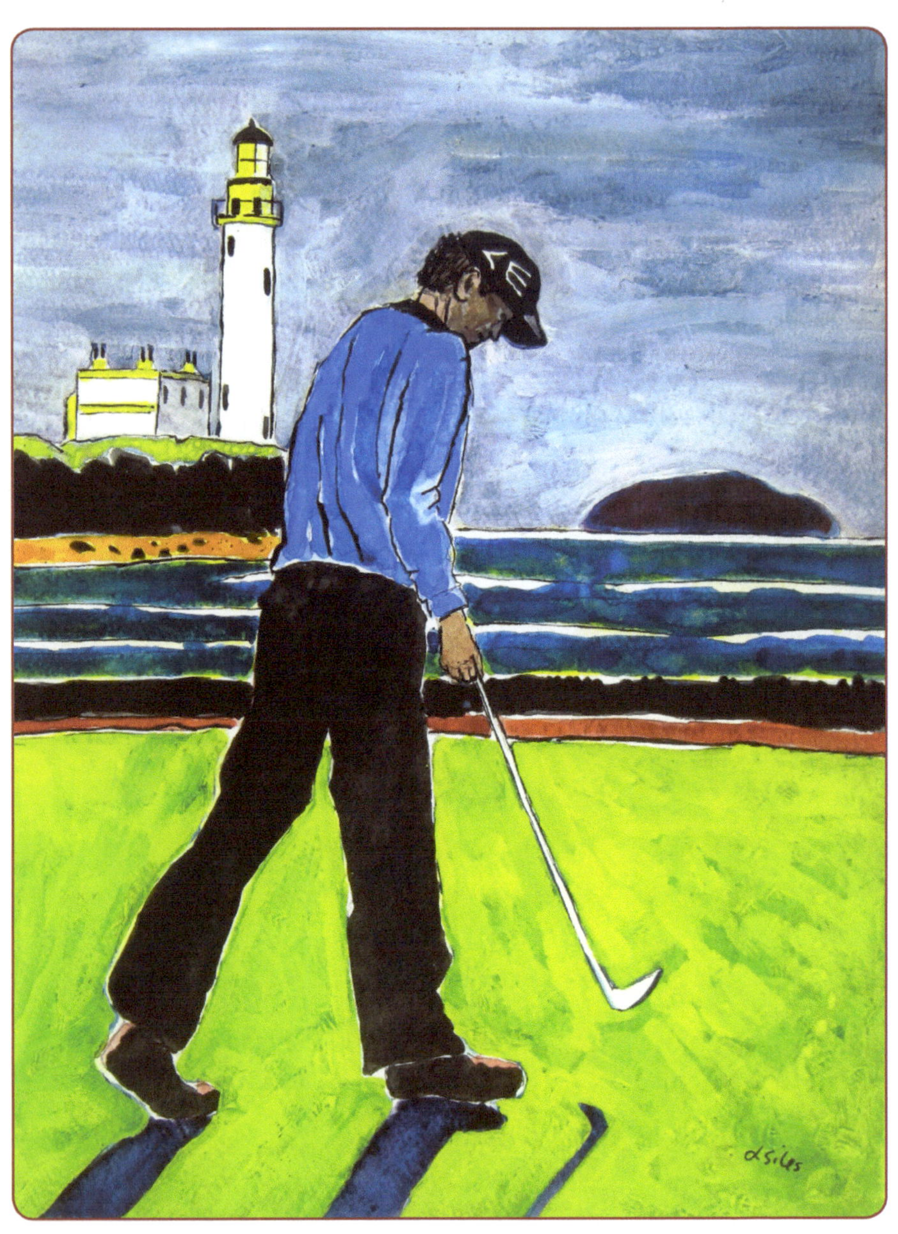

Lesley Giles

CHAPTER 1

That's Golf

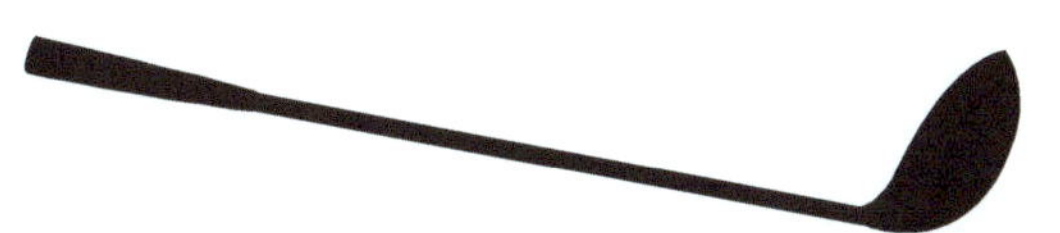

Golf is a good walk spoiled.

MARK TWAIN (1835-1910)

The pleasure I get from hitting the ball dead center on the club is comparable only to one or two other pleasures that come to mind.

DINAH SHORE (1916-1994)

A golfer is someone with hoof and mouth disease. He hoofs it all day and mouths it all night.

WILL ROGERS (1879-1935)

Welcome, grave stranger, to our green retreats,
Where health with exercise and freedom meets.

SIR WALTER SCOTT (1771-1832)

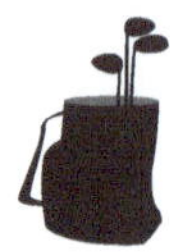

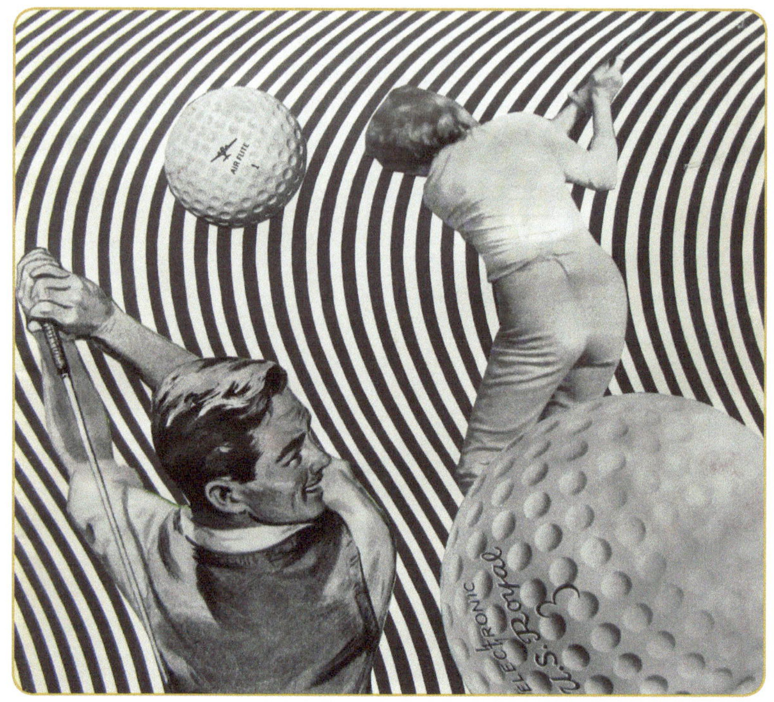

Shawn Marie Hardy

A good one iron shot is about as easy to come by as an understanding wife.

DAN JENKINS (b. 1929)

Golf is a lot like sex. It's something you can enjoy all your life. And if you remain an amateur, you get to pick your own playing partners.

JESS SWEETSER (1902-1989)

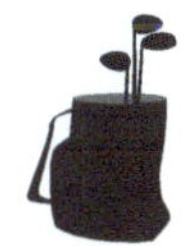

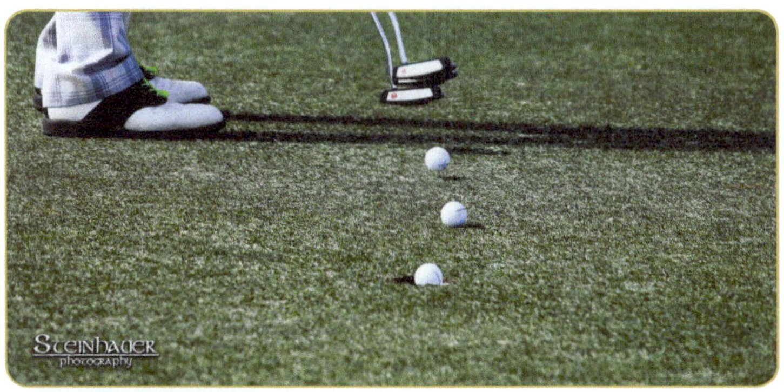

Tony Steinhauer

Golf, like measles, should be caught young,
for, if postponed to riper years,
the results may be serious.
P.G. WODEHOUSE (1881-1975)

Don Quixote would understand golf.
It is the impossible dream.
JIM MURRAY (1919-1998)

Golf is not a funeral,
though both can be very sad affairs.
BERNARD DARWIN (1876-1961)

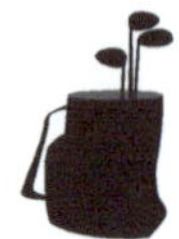

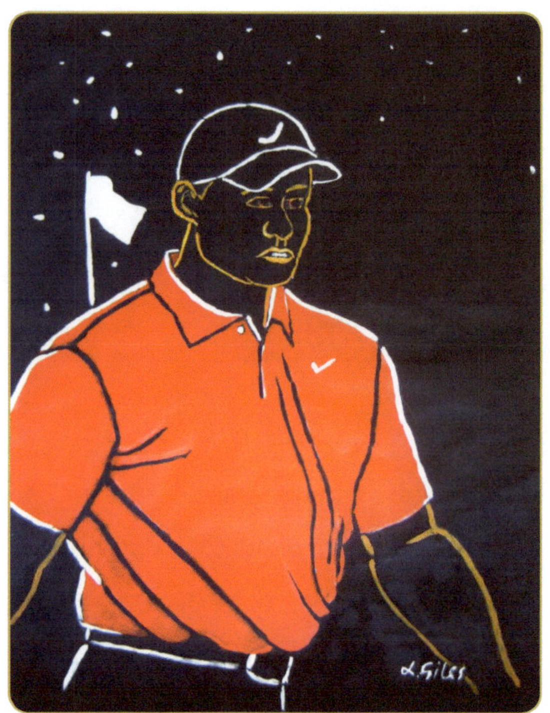

Lesley Giles

I beat Tiger Woods by five strokes—
he was only six at the time.

GREGG ZAUN (B. 1971)

And the wind shall say: Here were decent godless people. Their only monument the asphalt road. And a thousand lost golf balls.

T.S. ELIOT (1888-1965)

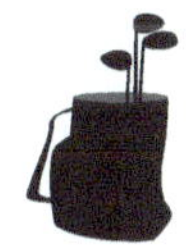

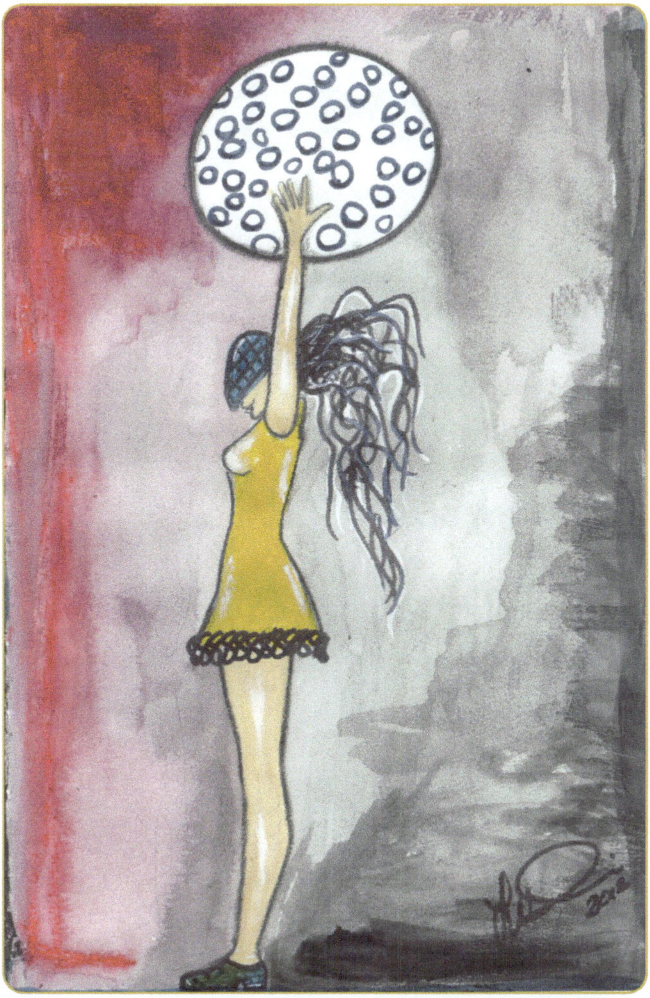

CHAPTER 1
That's Golf

Leslie Rodriguez

Just having fun. Got to do it while I've still got it.

TIGER WOODS (B. 1975)

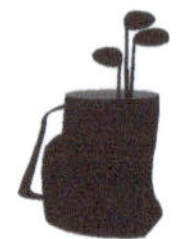

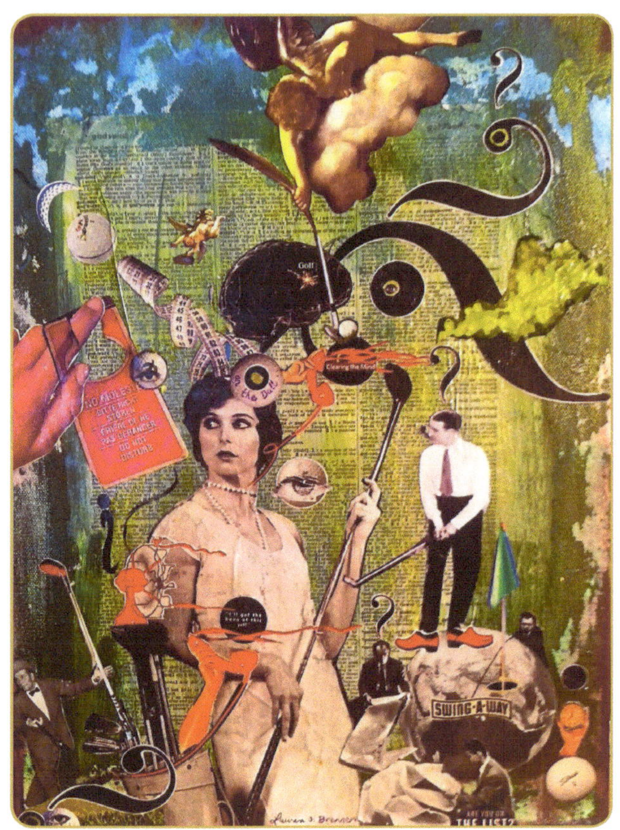

Lauren Brenner

I can only thank Davis Love III for turning me on to golf and showing me it isn't a sissy game.

MICHAEL JORDAN (b. 1963)

I'm the best. I just haven't played yet.

MUHAMMAD ALI (b. 1942)

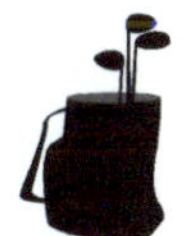

Happiness is a long walk with a putter in your hand.

WAYNE GRADY (b. 1957)

He enjoys that perfect peace, that peace beyond all understanding, which comes at its maximum only to the man who has given up golf.

P.G. WODEHOUSE (1881-1975)

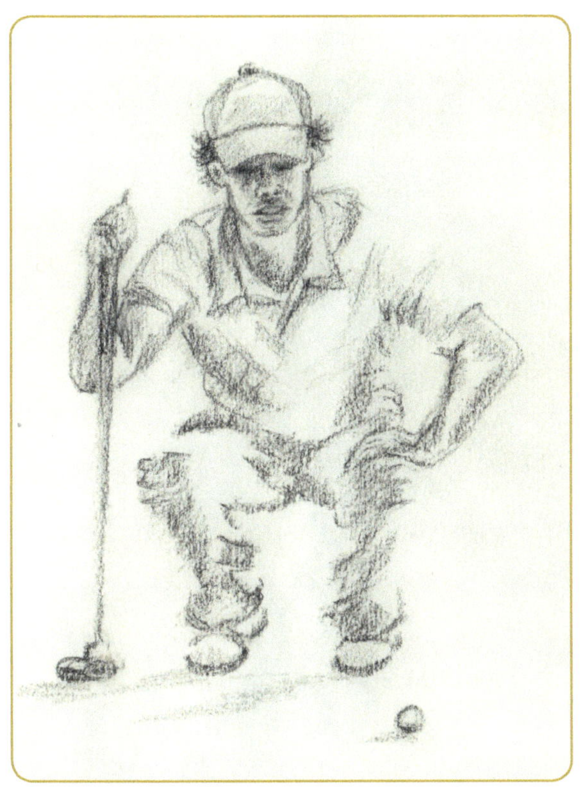

Paulette Farrell

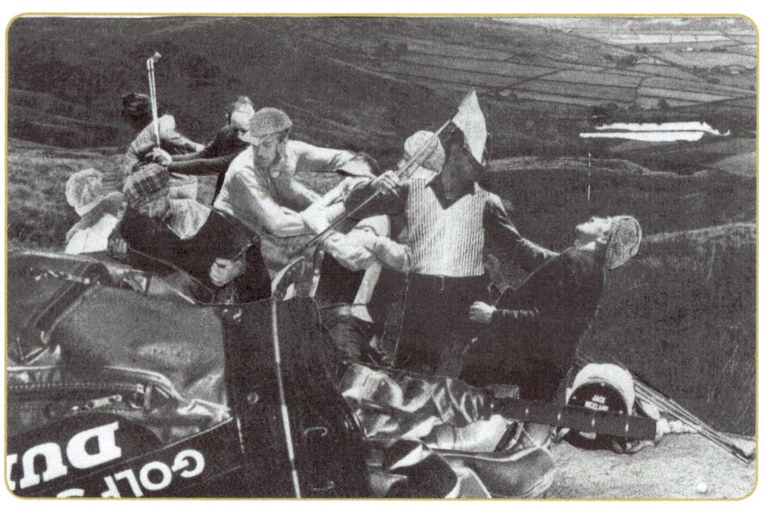

Ben Thompson

Playing golf is not hot work. Cutting sugar cane for a dollar a day—that's hot work.

CHI-CHI RODRIGUEZ (b. 1935)

I play in the low 80's.
If it's any hotter than that, I won't play.

JOE LOUIS (1914-1981)

The best wood in most amateurs' bags is the pencil.

CHI-CHI RODRIGUEZ (b. 1935)

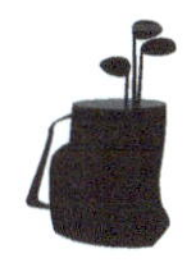

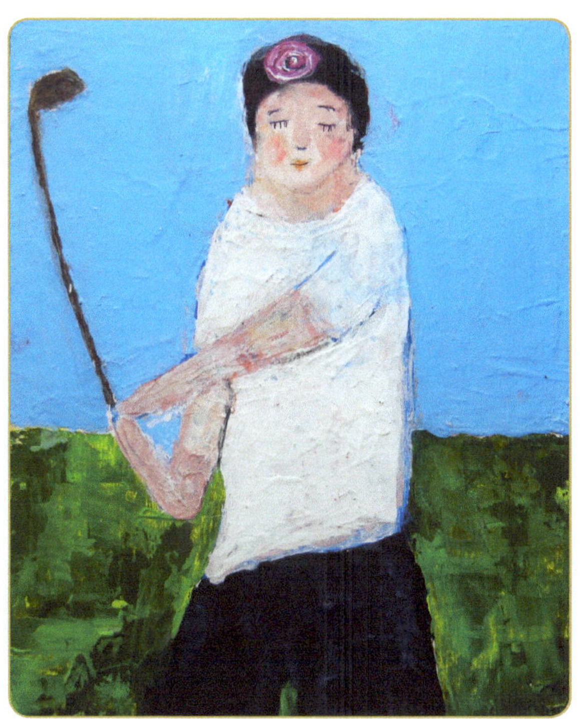

Katherine Wood

Golf is the only game where the worst player gets the best of it. He gets more out of it with regard to both exercise and enjoyment.

DAVID LLOYD GEORGE (1863-1945)

Whoever plays with a club shall be fined 20 shillings or their upper garment.

THE MAGISTRATE OF BRUSSELS (1360)

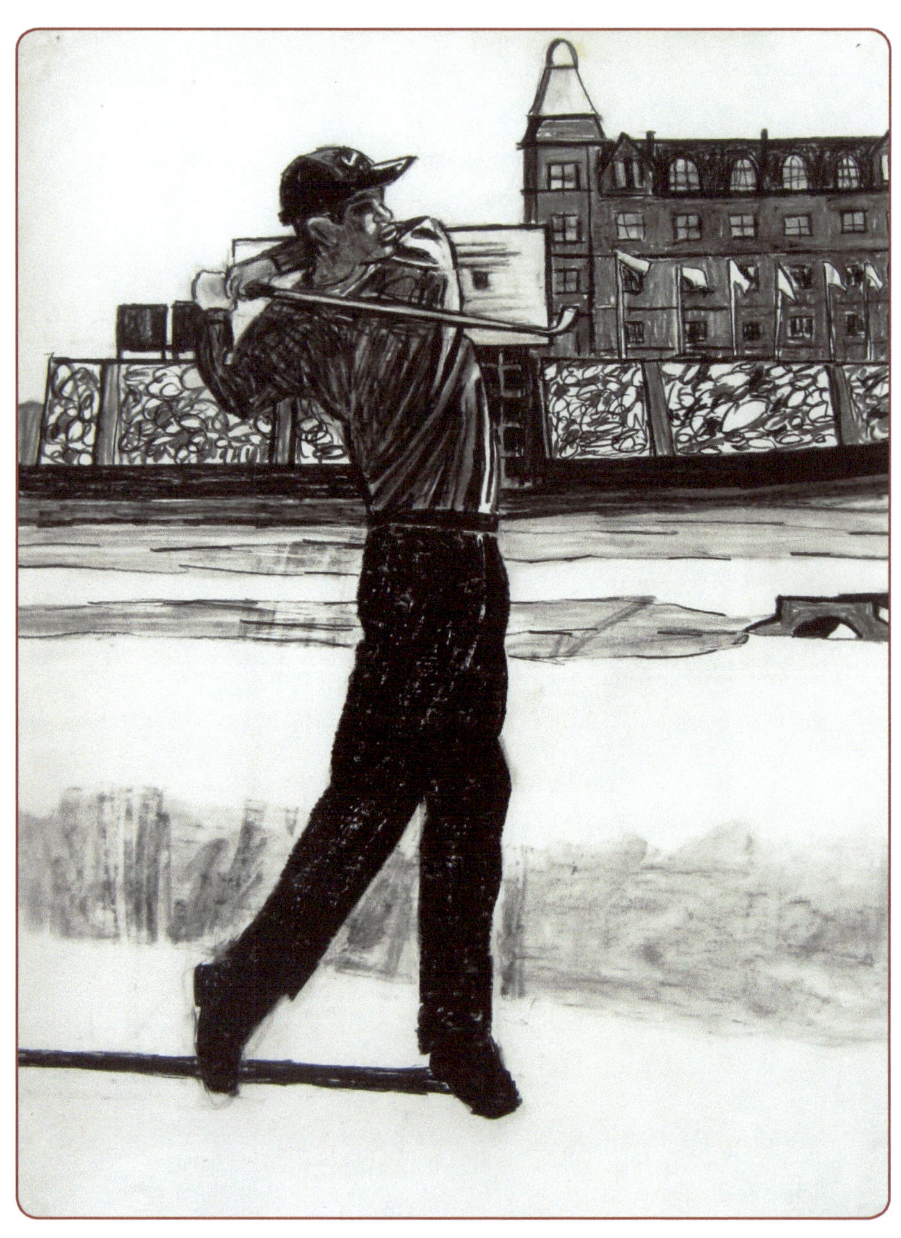

Lesley Giles

CHAPTER 2

The Pros

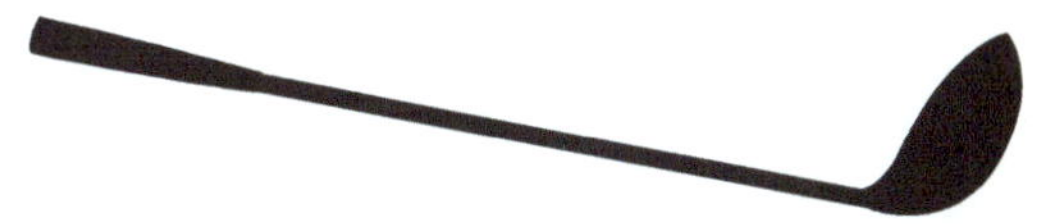

Golf is a puzzle without an answer.
I've played the game for 40 years and I still
haven't the slightest idea how to play.

GARY PLAYER (b. 1935)

"To be truthful, I think golfers are overpaid.
It's unreal, and I have trouble dealing with
the guilt sometimes"

COLIN MONTGOMERIE (b. 1963)

The dollars aren't important . . .once you have them.

JOHNNY MILLER (b. 1947)

The first time I grabbed a golf club, I knew that
I'd do it for the rest of my life.

MICHELLE WIE (b. 1989)

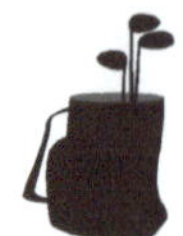

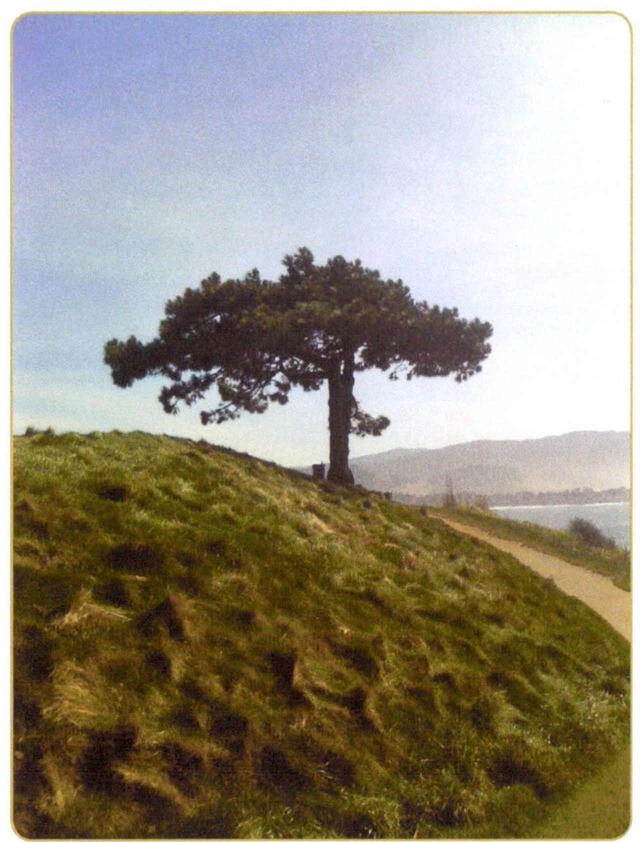

Julie Wheler

The simpler I keep things, the better I play.

NANCY LOPEZ (b. 1957)

You can talk to a fade but a hook won't listen.

LEE TREVINO (b. 1939)

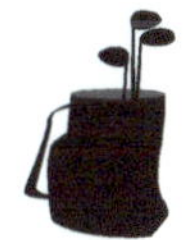

I owe everything to golf. Where else would a guy with an IQ like mine make this much money?

HUBERT GREEN (b. 1946)

Professional golf is the only sport where, if you win twenty percent of the time, you're the best.

JACK NICKLAUS (b. 1940)

"I owe a lot to my parents, especially my mother and father."

GREG NORMAN (b. 1955)

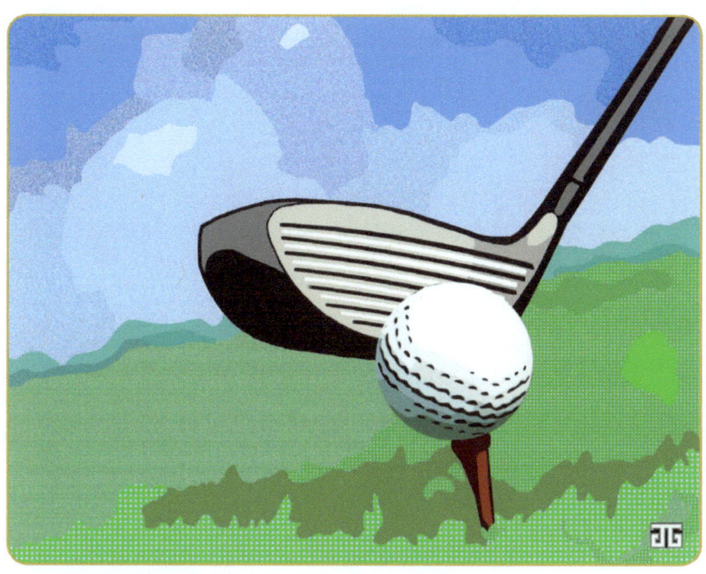

Jesse Glenn

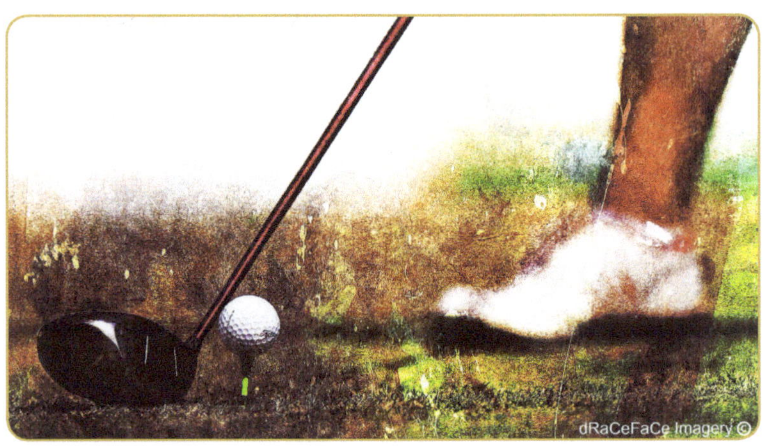

Drace Brown

How long does John Daly drive a golf ball? When I was a kid, I didn't go that far on vacation.

CHI-CHI RODRIGUEZ (b. 1935)

I learned you can't drink whiskey and play golf.

JOHN DALY (b. 1966)

Do I have to know rules and all that crap? Then forget it.

JOHN DALY (b. 1966)

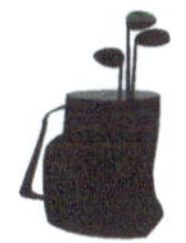

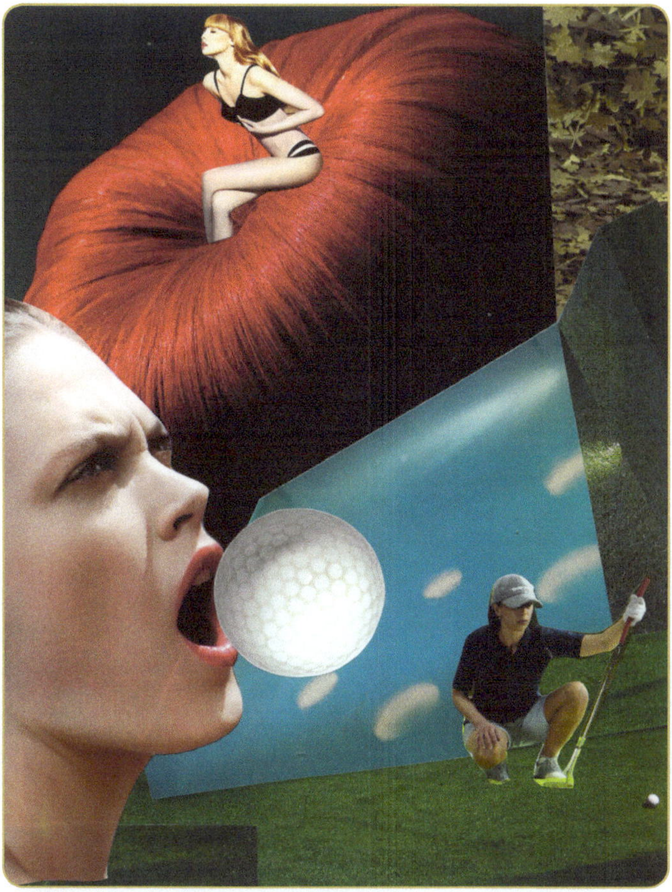

Mongobi-Bibbiana T. Mele

I just love American girls. That is a big attraction for me over here. The girls have class and are incredibly beautiful.

SERGIO GARCIA (b. 1980)

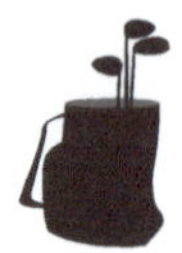

Peter Alliss used to say I hit miracle shots. I never thought that. Miracles don't happen very often; I was hitting those shots all the time.

SEVE BALLESTEROS (1957-2011)

The best year of my life was when I was eleven. I got straight As, had two recesses a day, and the cutest girlfriend, and won thirty-two tournaments that year. Everything's been downhill since.

TIGER WOODS (b. 1975)

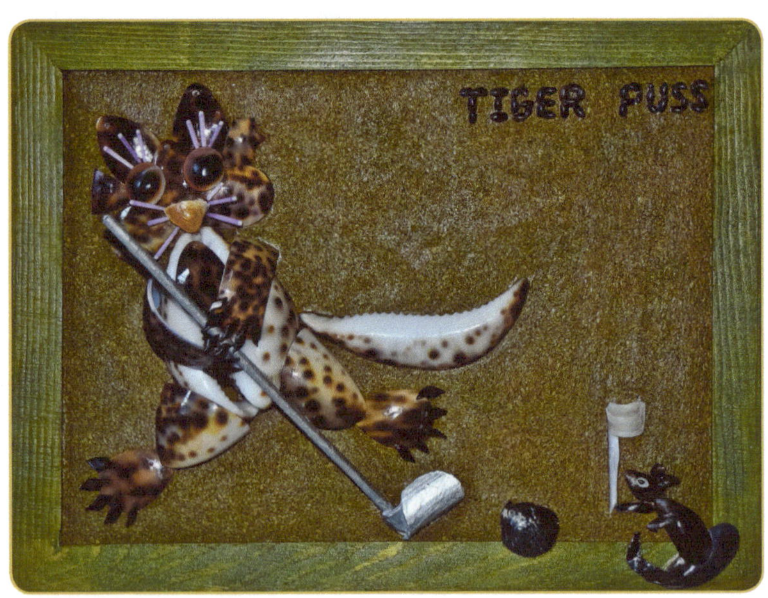

Alla Baksanskaya

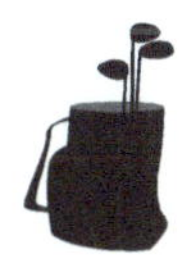

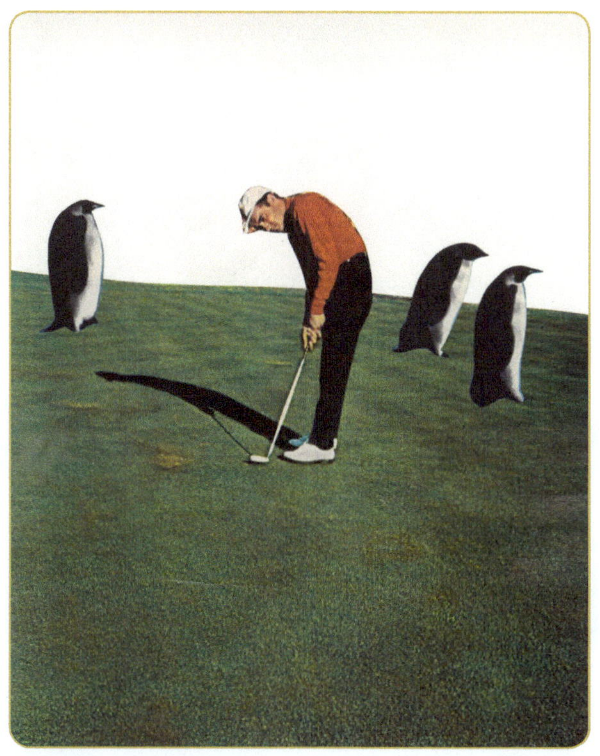

Marian Williams

Q: Thirteen? How the hell did you make 13 on a par-5?
Arnold Palmer: Missed a 12-footer for 12.

ARNOLD PALMER (b. 1929)

Some people say I play erratic golf.
What they mean is I frequently play lousy.

TOM SHAW (b. 1938)

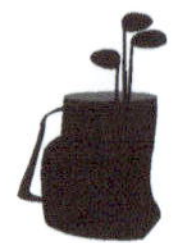

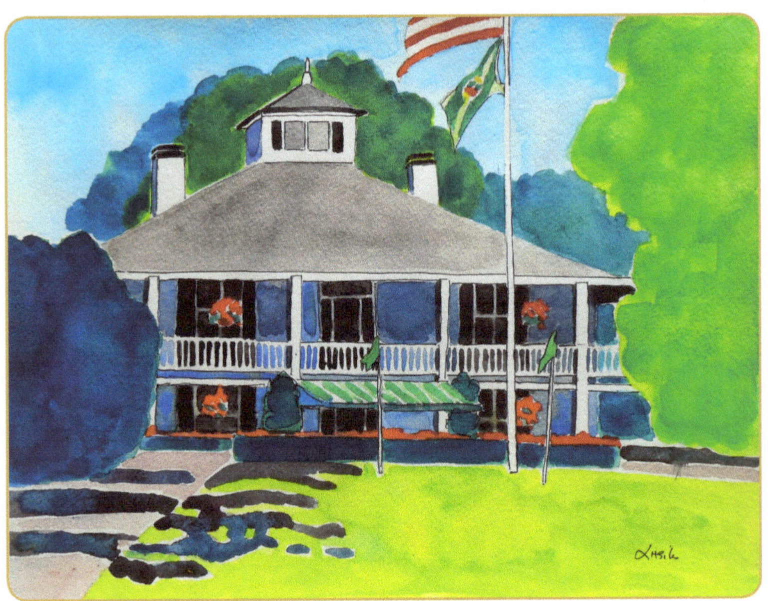

Lesley Giles

You start to choke at the Masters when
you drive through the front gate.

HALE IRWIN (b. 1945)

The first time I played the Masters,
I was so nervous I drank a bottle of rum before
I teed off. I shot the happiest 83 of my life.

CHI-CHI RODRIGUEZ (b. 1935)

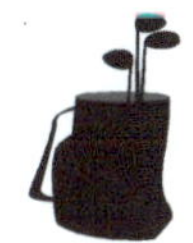

For an amateur, standing on the first hole of the Masters is the ultimate laxative.

TREVOR HOMER (b. 195?)

"These greens are so fast I have to hold my putter over the ball and hit it with the shadow."

SAM SNEAD (1912-2002)

At Augusta National they bikini-wax the greens.

GARY McCORD (b. 1948)

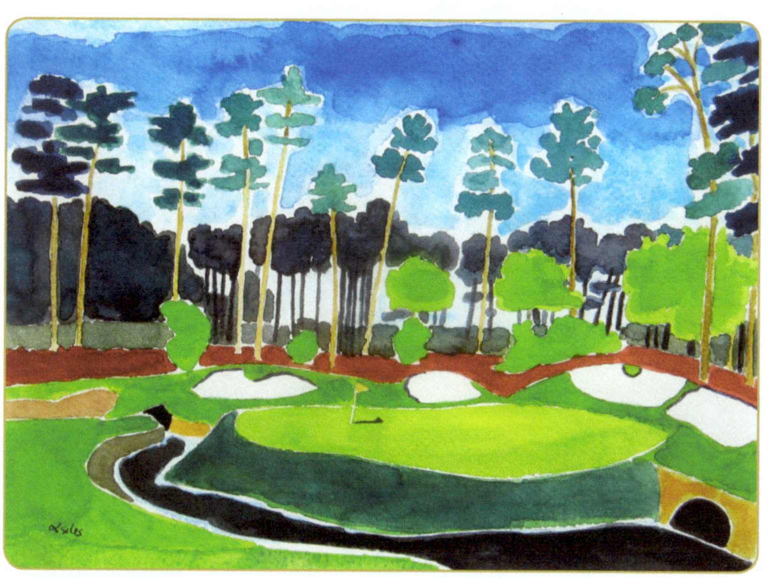

Lesley Giles

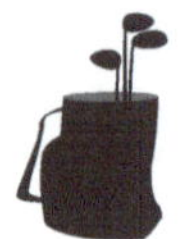

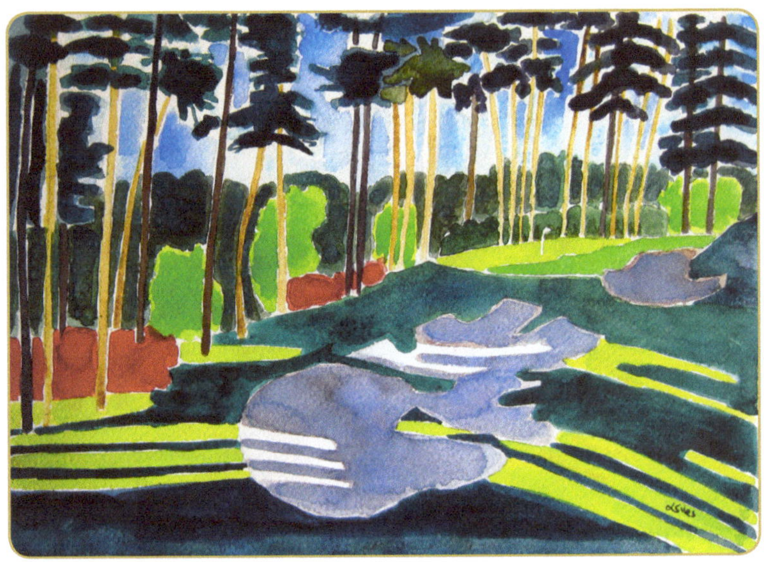

Lesley Giles

There is absolutely nothing humorous
at the Masters. Here, small dogs do not
bark and babies do not cry.

GARY PLAYER (b. 1935)

I've never been to Heaven, and thinkin' back on
my life, I probably won't get a chance to go.
I guess the Masters is as close as I am going to get.

FUZZY ZOELLER (b. 1951)

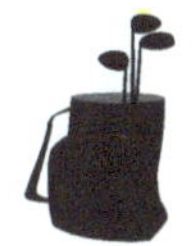

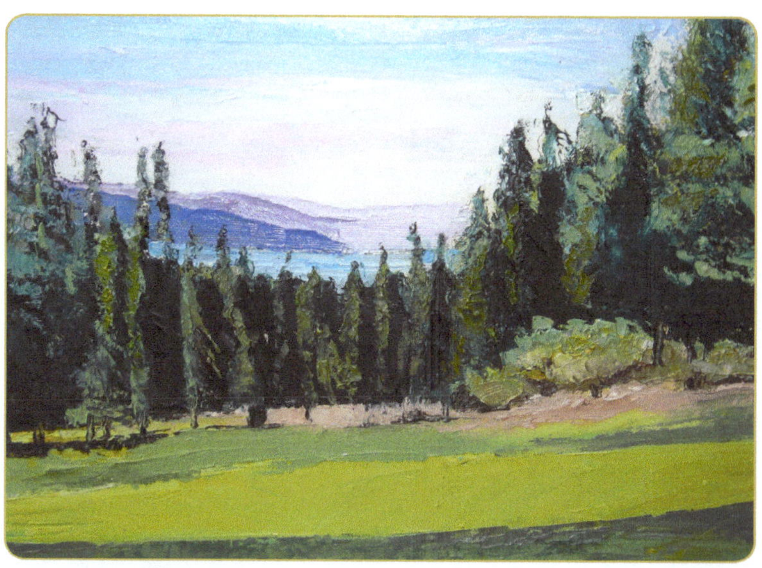

Christine LaGrow

Always count your blessings. Be thankful you are able to be out on a beautiful course. Most people in the world don't have that opportunity.

FRED COUPLES (b. 1959)

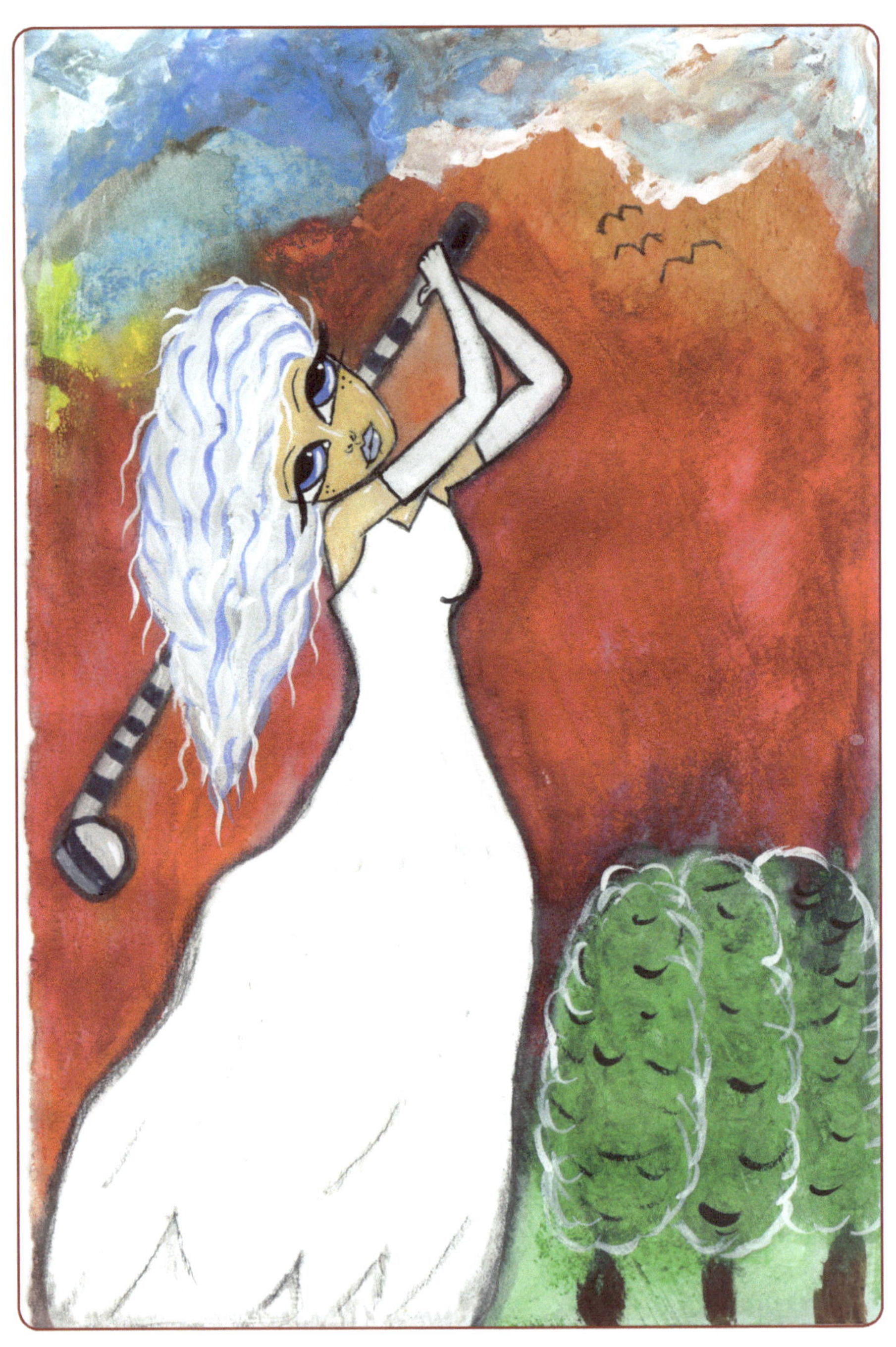

Leslie Rodriguez

CHAPTER 3

Golf Humor

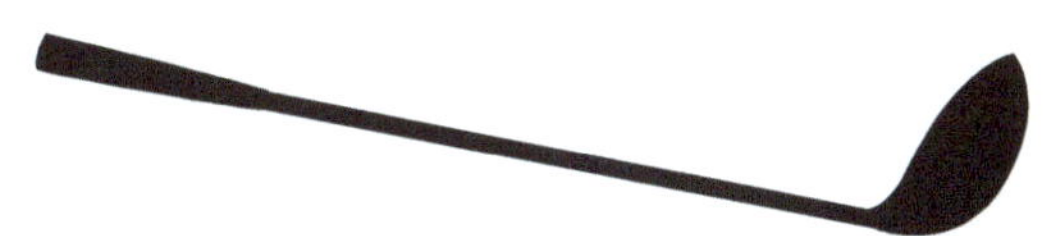

Golf is the most fun you can have
without taking your clothes off.

CHI-CHI RODRIGUEZ (b. 1935)

I asked my wife, Gill, if she wanted a Versace dress, diamonds, or pearls as a present and she said no. When I asked her what she did want, she said: 'A divorce,' but I told her I wasn't planning to spend that much.

NICK FALDO (b. 1957)

Golf is typical capitalist lunacy.

GEORGE BERNARD SHAW (1856-1950)

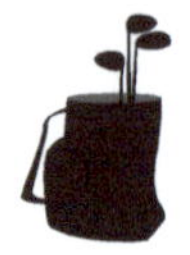

The game of choice for unemployed people or maintenance level workers is basketball.
The game of choice for frontline workers is football.
The game of choice for middle management is tennis.
The game of choice for CEOs and executives is golf.
Conclusion: The higher up on the ladder you are, the smaller your balls are.

ANONYMOUS

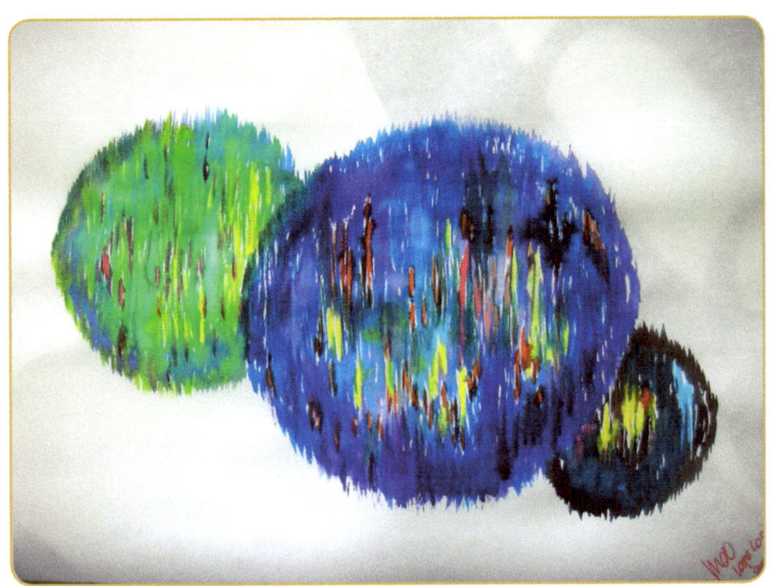

Moo Monika Mori

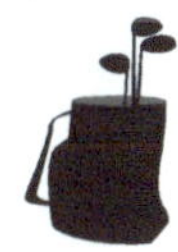

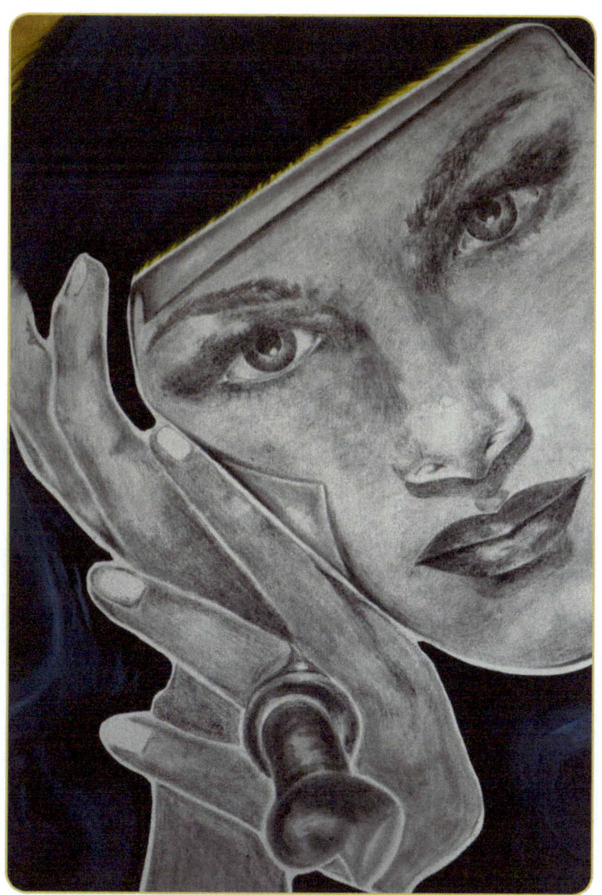

Marlene Jorge

Golf is very much like a love affair:
if you don't take it seriously, it's no fun;
if you do, it breaks your heart.

LOUISE SUGGS (b. 1923)

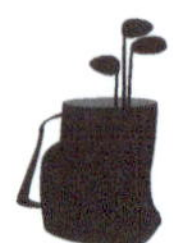

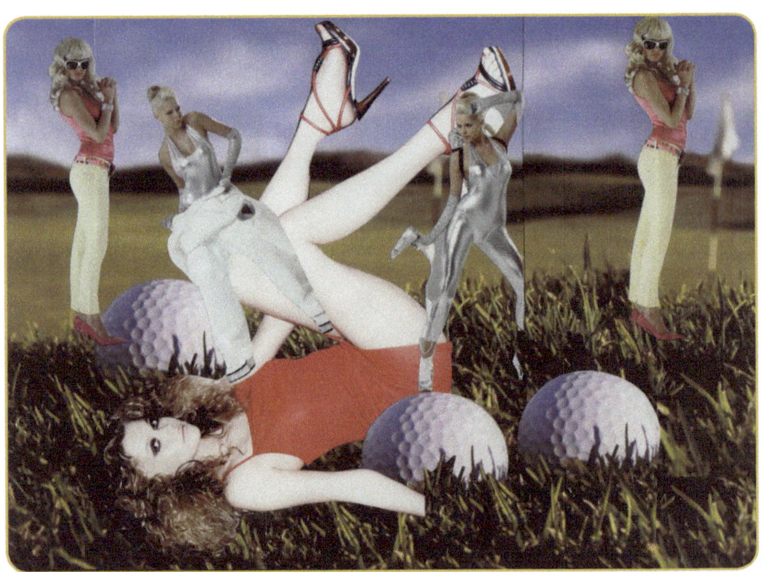

Mongobi-Bibbiana T. Mele

After a golfer has been out on the circuit for a while he learns how to handle his dating so that it doesn't interfere with his golf. The first rule usually is no woman-chasing after Wednesday.

TONY LEMA (1932-1966)

You can make a lot of money in this game. Just ask my ex-wives. Both of them are so rich that neither of their husbands work.

LEE TREVINO (b. 1939)

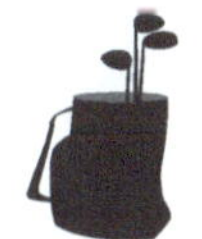

Hockey is a sport for white men.
Basketball is a sport for black men, Golf is a sport
for white men dressed like black pimps.

TIGER WOODS (b. 1975)

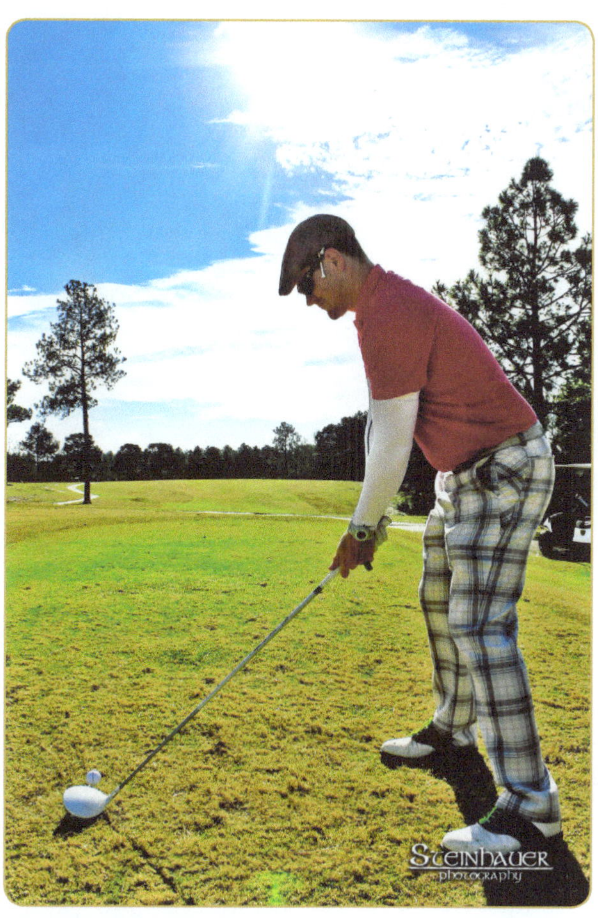

Tony Steinhauer

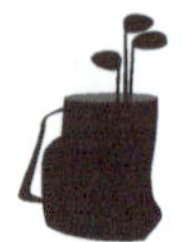

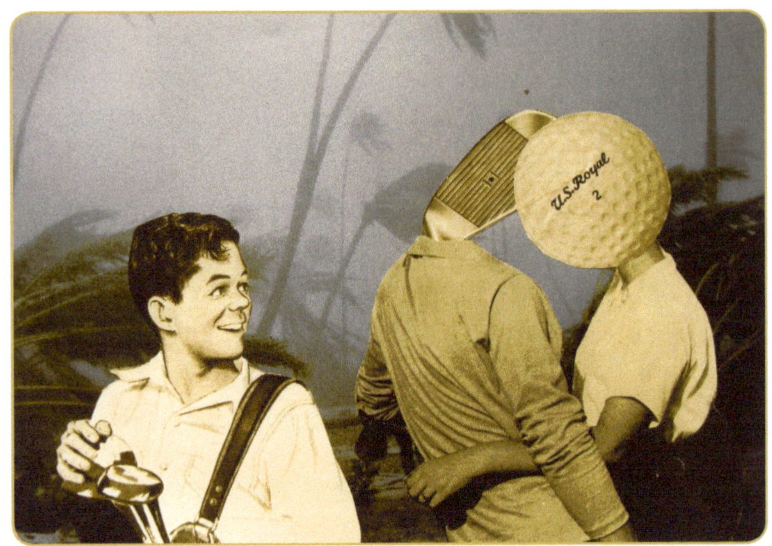

Shawn Marie Hardy

I'm not feeling well—I need a doctor immediately.
Ring the nearest golf course.

GROUCHO MARX (1890-1977)

If you drink, don't drive. Don't even putt.

DEAN MARTIN (1917-1995)

Golf and sex are the only things you
can enjoy without being good at them.

JIMMY DEMARET (1910-1983)

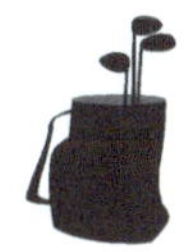

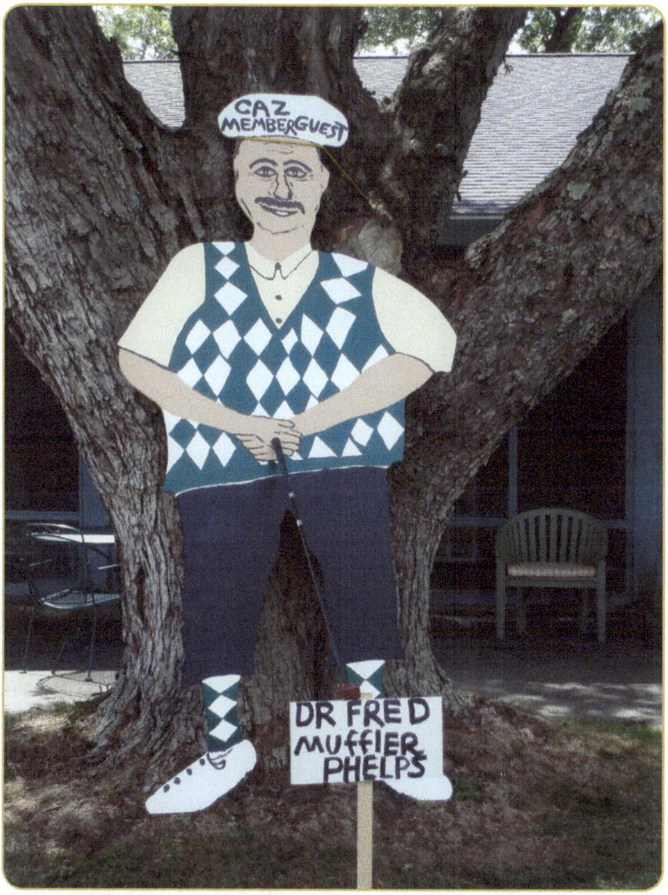

Charles Andrews

Golf and women are a lot alike. You know you are not going to wind up with anything but grief, but you can't resist the impulse.

JACKIE GLEASON (1916-1987)

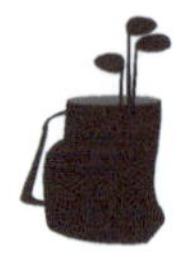

The difference between golf and the government is that in golf you can't improve your life.

GEORGE DEUKMEHAN (b. 1928)

Last week Arnold Palmer told me how I could cut eight strokes off my score. He'd say, 'Skip one of the par 3s.'

BOB HOPE (1903-2003)

Golf . . . a young man's vice and an old man's penance.

IRVIN S. COBB (1876-1944)

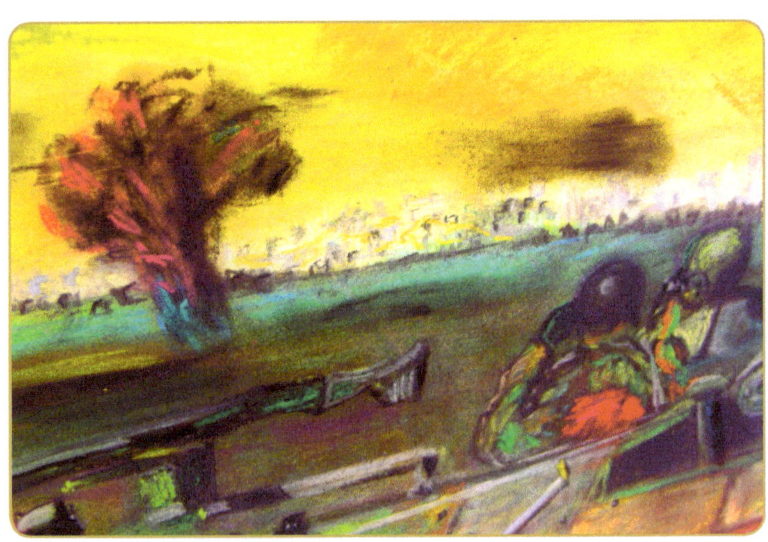

Lior Immanuel Fischer

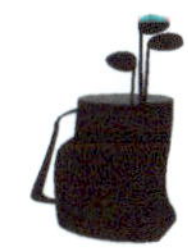

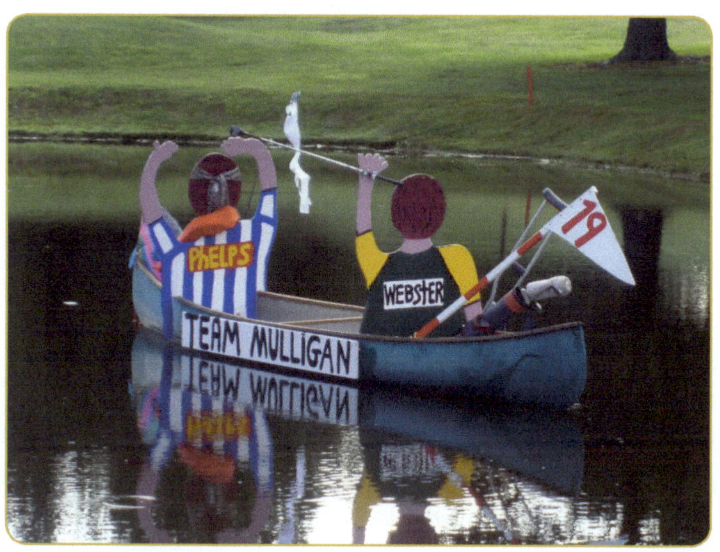

Charles Andrews

Mulligan: invented by an Irishman who wanted to hit one more 20-yard grounder.

JIM BISHOP (1907-1987)

Golf is a game in which you yell 'fore,' shoot six, and write down five.

PAUL HARVEY (1918-2009)

They call it golf because all of the other four-letter words were taken.

RAYMOND FLOYD (b. 1942)

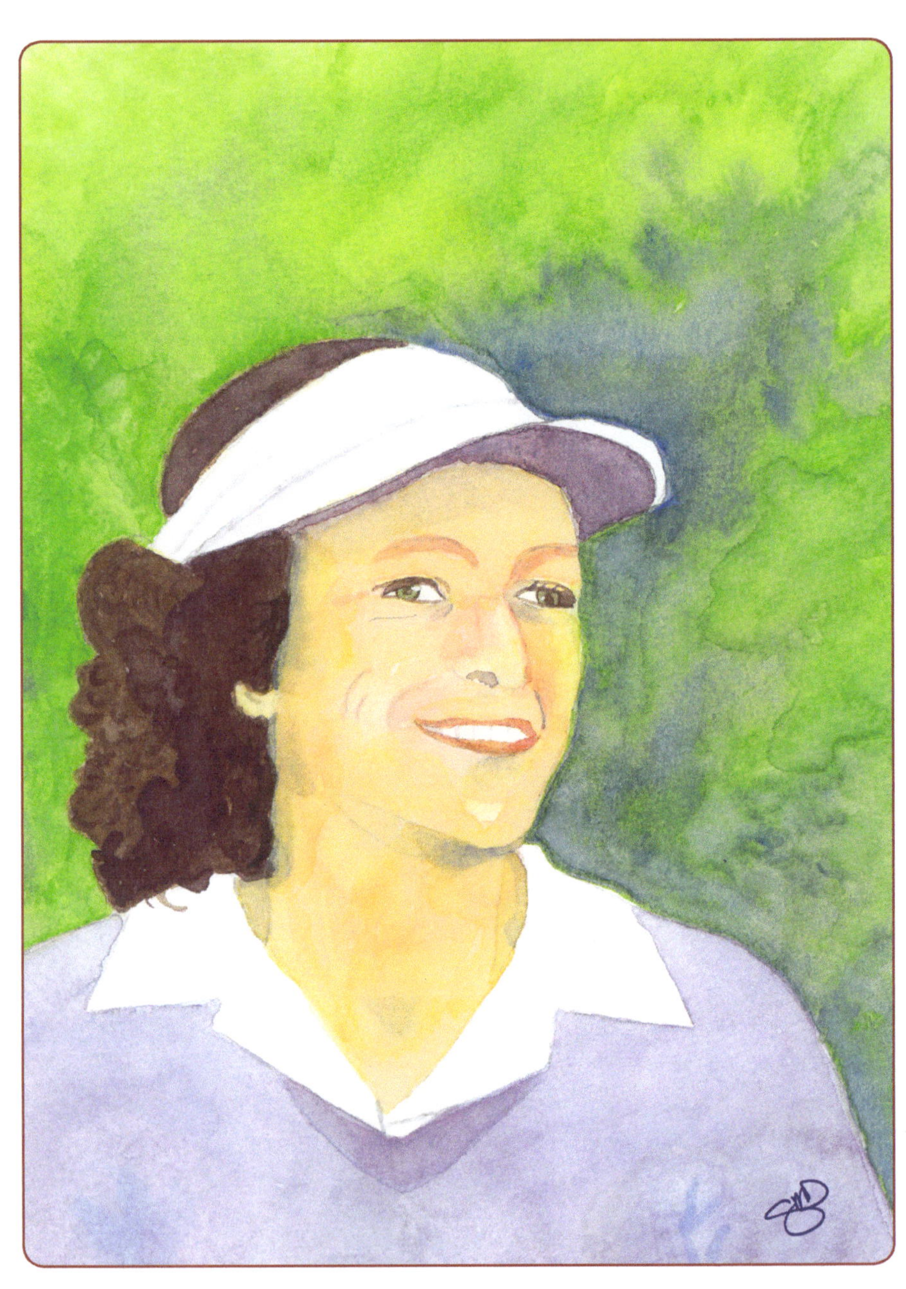

Sheila Delgado

CHAPTER 4

Winning & Losing

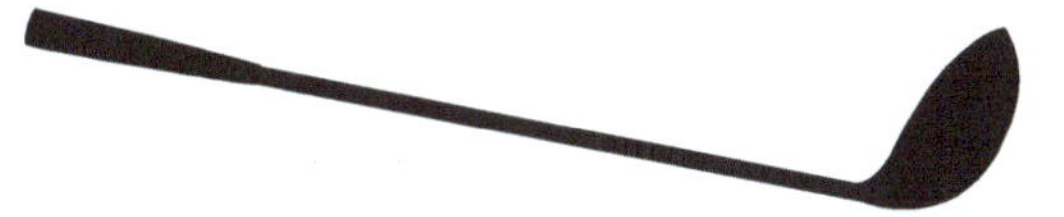

It's not whether you win or lose—
but whether I win or lose.

SANDY LYLE (b. 1958)

A lot of guys who have never choked have
never been in the position to do so.

TOM WATSON (b. 1949)

I don't fear death, but I sure don't like
those three-footers for par.

CHI-CHI RODRIGUEZ (b. 1935)

The object of golf is not just to win.
It is to play like a gentleman, and win.

PHIL MICKELSON (b. 1970)

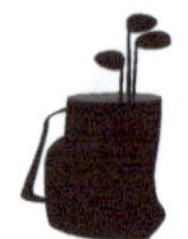

Forget your opponents; always play against par.

SAM SNEAD (1912-2002)

If you want to increase your success rate,
double your failure rate.

TOM WATSON (b. 1949)

Winning isn't everything, but wanting it is.

ARNOLD PALMER (b. 1929)

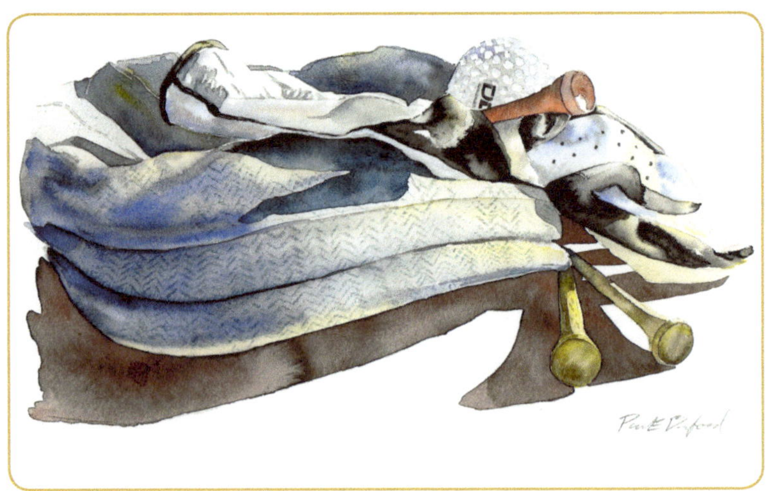

Paul Buford

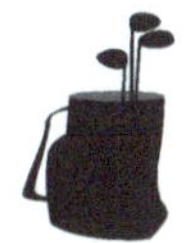

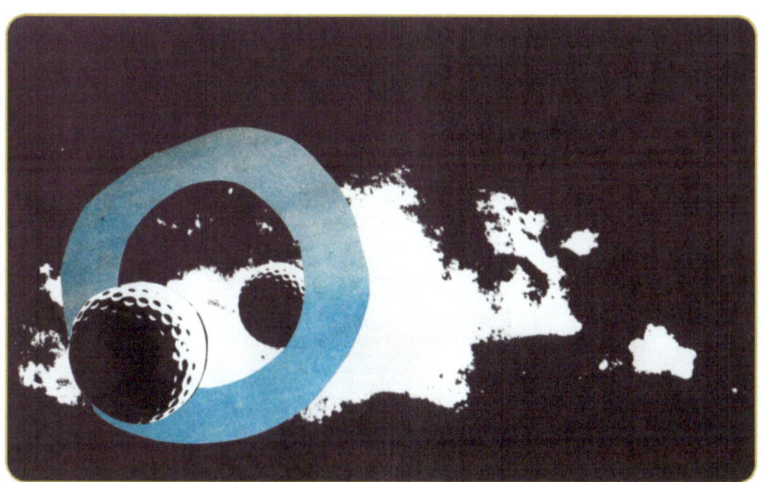

Marian Williams

Golf is a game of days,
and I can beat anyone on my day.

FUZZY ZOELLER (b. 1951)

When you play the game for fun, it's fun. When you play it for a living, it's a game of sorrows.

GARY PLAYER (b. 1935)

Competitors take bad breaks and use them to drive themselves just that much harder. Quitters take bad breaks and use them as reasons to give up.

NANCY LOPEZ (b. 1957)

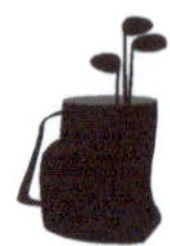

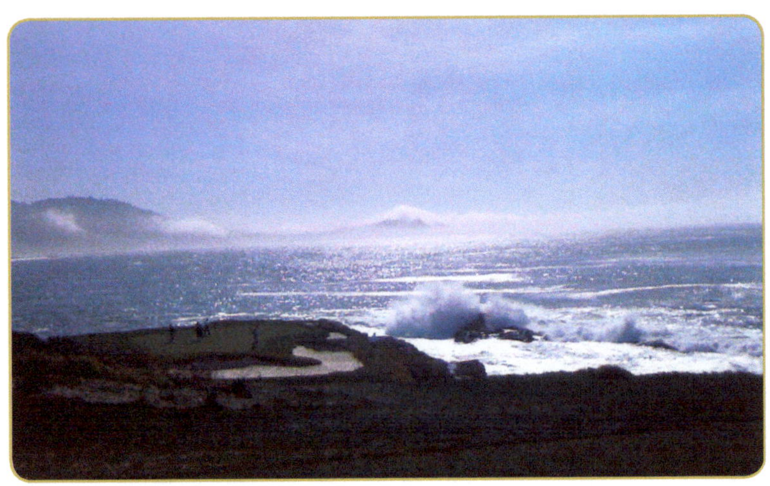

Julie Wheler

How can they beat me? I've been struck by lightning, had two back operations, and been divorced twice.

LEE TREVINO (b. 1939)

Pressure is playing for $50 a hole with only $5 in your pocket.

LEE TREVINO (b. 1939)

Man, this is one of them airport drivers. That's right. You hit this thing for two days, miss the cut, and go to the airport.

LEE TREVINO (b. 1939)

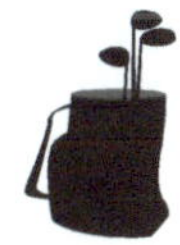

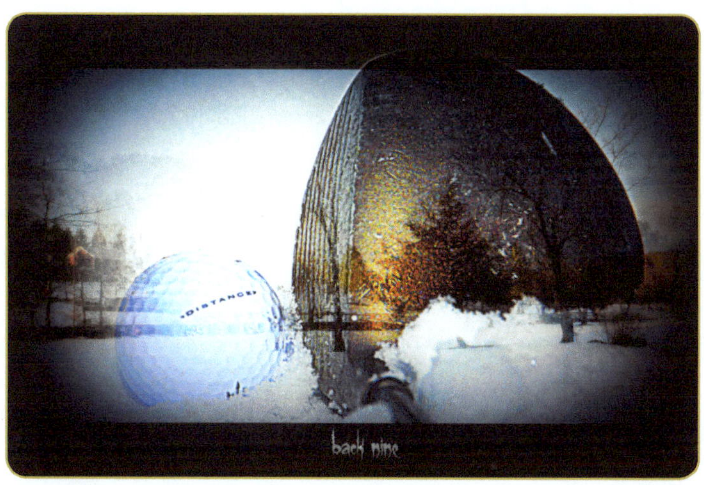

Earl Devendorf

The word is control.
That's my ultimate—to have control.
NICK FALDO (b. 1957)

I know there's a lot of guys who would love to see me fail. Well, good. Let 'em. I'm glad.
JOHN DALY (b. 1966)

If you want to beat someone out on the golf course, just get him mad.
DAVE WILLIAMS (1918-1998)

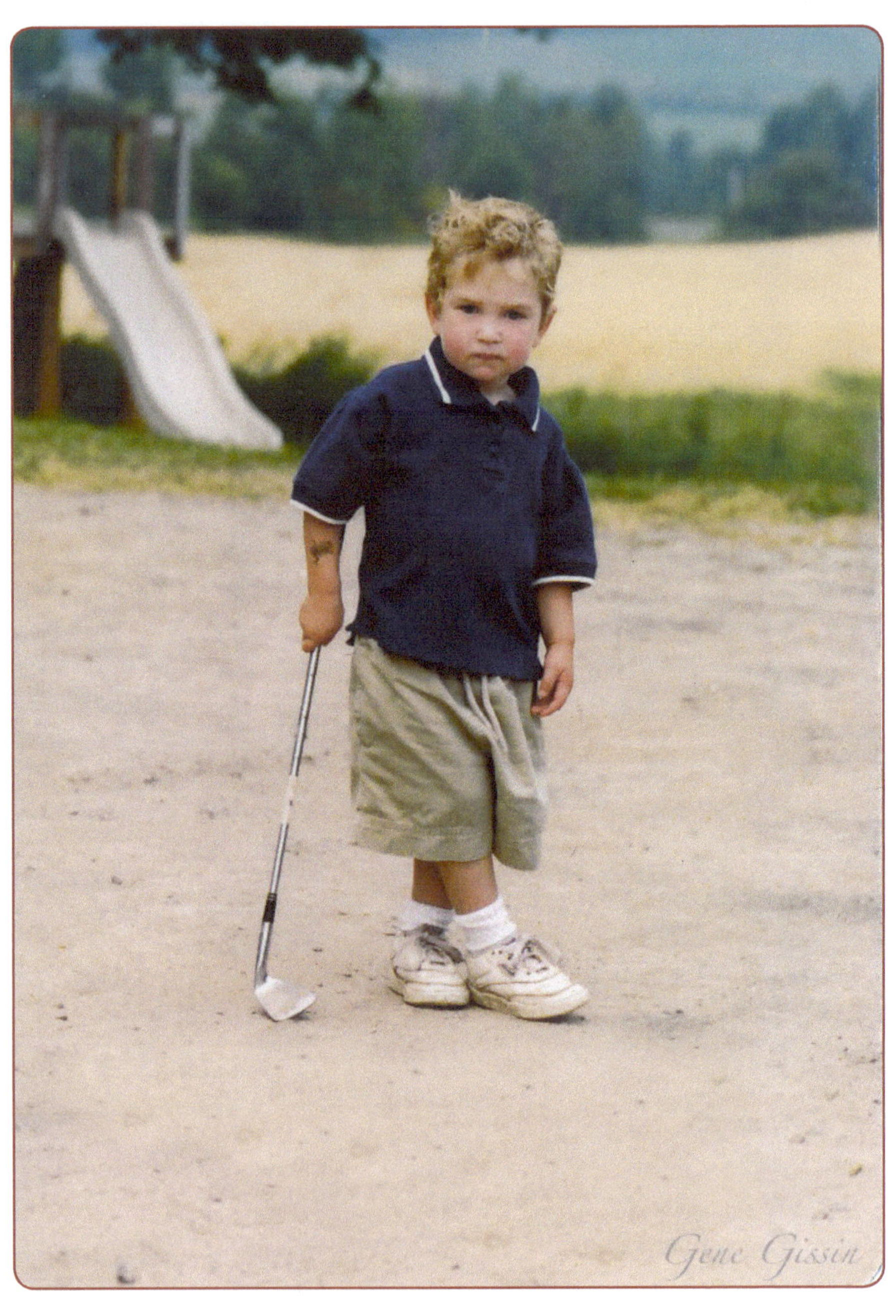

Gene Gissin

CHAPTER 5

Sportsmanship

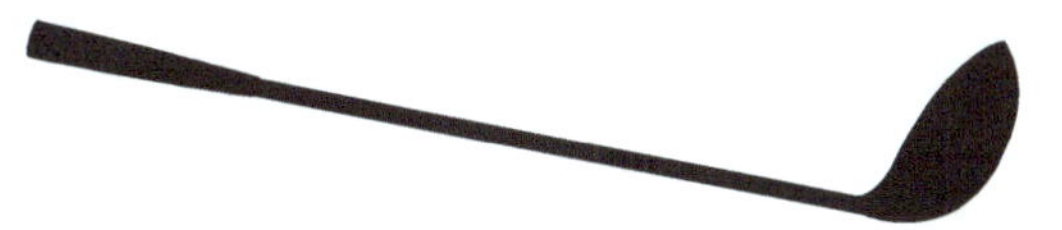

It's good sportsmanship to not pick up lost golf balls while they are still rolling.

MARK TWAIN (1835-1910)

I have often been gratefully aware of the heroic efforts of my opponent not to laugh at me.

BERNARD DARWIN (1876-1961)

One reward golf has given me, and I shall always be thankful for it, is introducing me to some of the world's most picturesque, tireless, and bald-faced liars.

RING LARDNER (1885-1933)

Is my friend in the bunker or is the bastard on the green?

PETER DONOHOE (b. 1947)

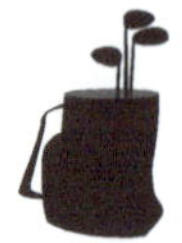

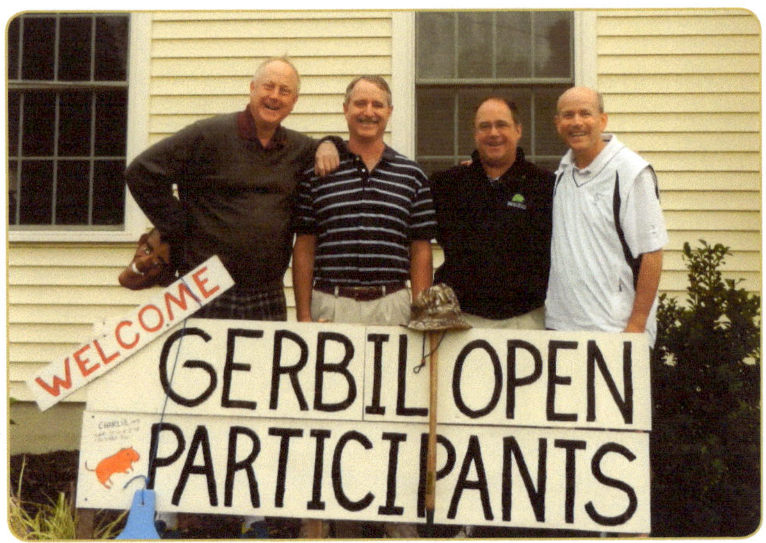

Charles Andrews

But in the end it's still a game of golf,
and if at the end of the day you can't shake
hands with your opponents and still be friends,
then you've missed the point.

PAYNE STEWART (1957-1999)

When you die, what you take with you is what
you leave behind. If you don't share, no matter
how much you have, you will always be poor.

CHI-CHI RODRIGUEZ (b. 1935)

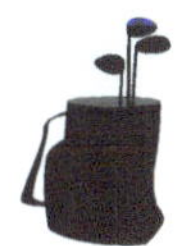

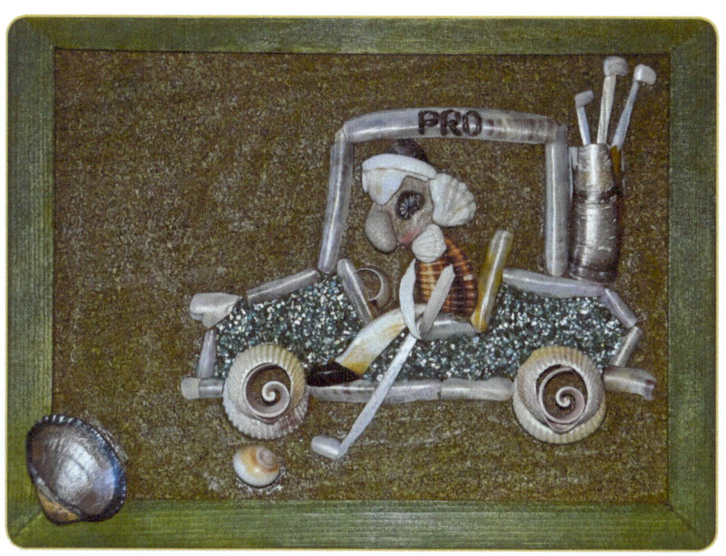

Alla Baksanskaya

You know the old rule: He who has the fastest cart never has to play a bad lie.

MICKEY MANTLE (1931-1995)

Why am I using a new putter? Because the last one didn't float.

CRAIG STADLER (b. 1953)

He (George Meany) plays just like a union man. He negotiates the final score.

BOB HOPE (1903-2003)

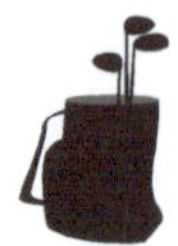

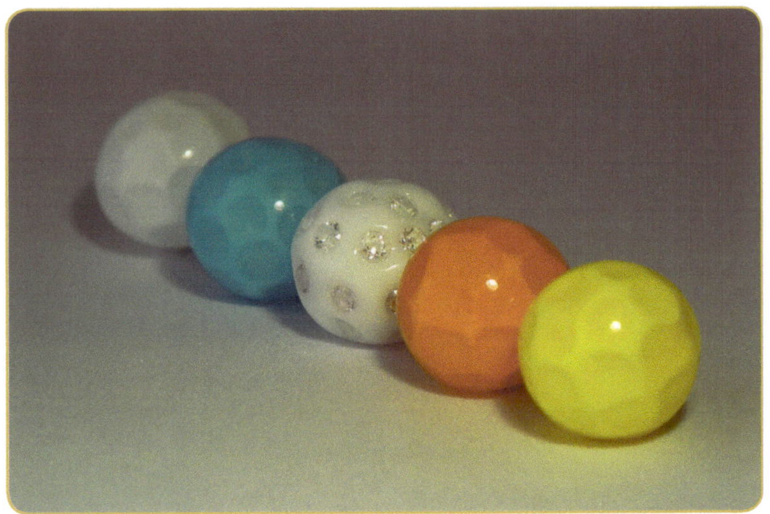

Leslie Foster

If you call on God to improve the results of a shot while it is still in motion, you are using 'an outside agency' and subject to appropriate penalties under the rules of golf.

HENRY LONGHURST (1909-1978)

Golf is the only game in which a precise knowledge of the rules can earn one a reputation for bad sportsmanship.

PATRICK CAMPBELL (1913-1980)

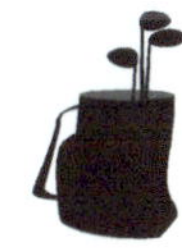

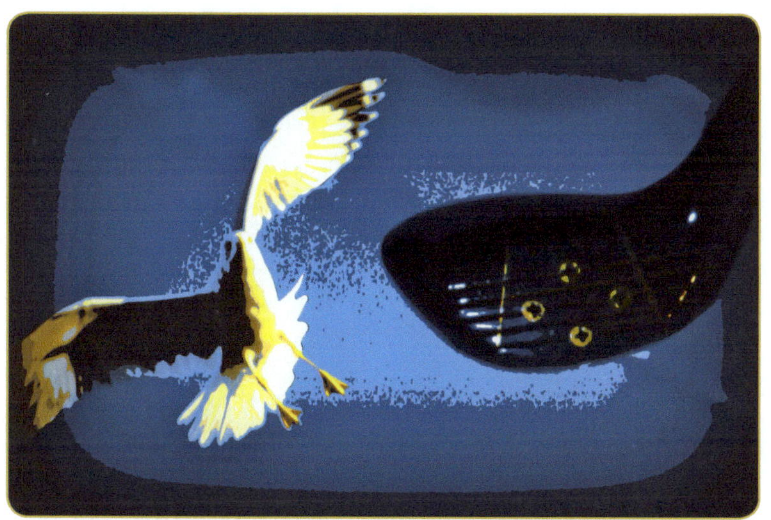

Earl Devendorf

Old-time golfers insist that there is nothing more satisfying in the game of golf than the crisp snap of a hickory-shafted club breaking sharply across the player's knee.

HENRY BEARD (b. 1945)

You get to know more of the character of a man in a round of golf than in six months of political experience.

DAVID LLOYD GEORGE (1863-1945)

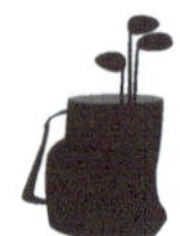

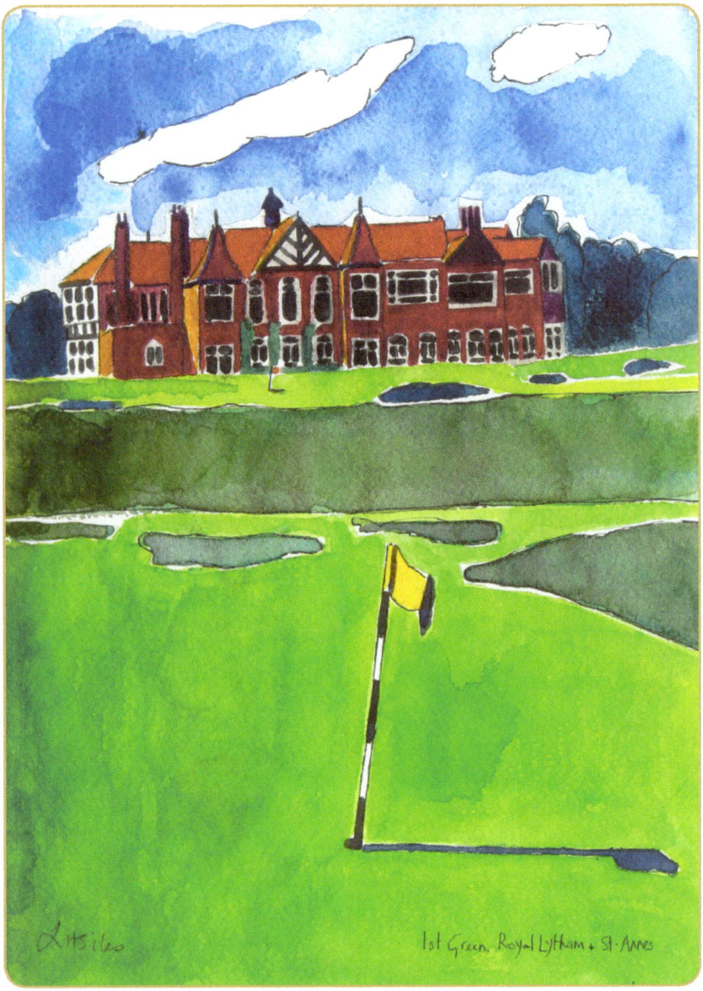

Lesley Giles

Golf is a game not just of manners but of morals.

ART SPANDER (b. 1938)

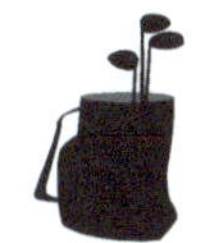

To many, Bolt's putter has spent
more time in the air than Lindbergh.

JIMMY DEMARET (1910-1983)

If you are going to throw a club, it is important to throw it ahead of you, down the fairway, so you don't have to waste energy going back to pick it up.

TOMMY BOLT (1916-2008)

Bolt (to caddie): Why are you handling me a 3-iron for a shot of less than 100 yards?
Caddie (nervously): Because it's the only club left.

TOMMY BOLT (1916-2008)

I never cussed much. That's a bunch of bullshit.

TOMMY BOLT (1916-2008)

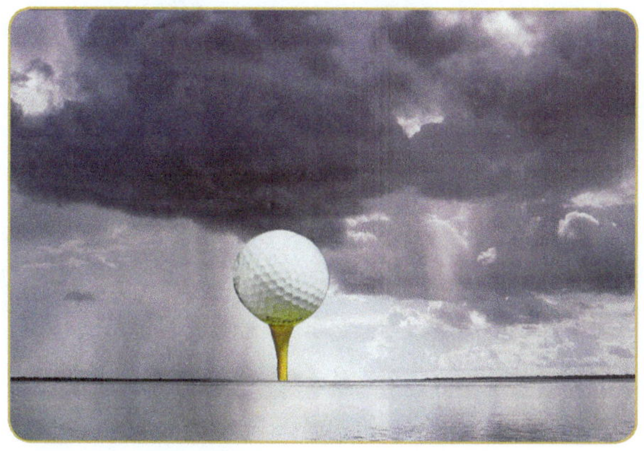

Marian Williams

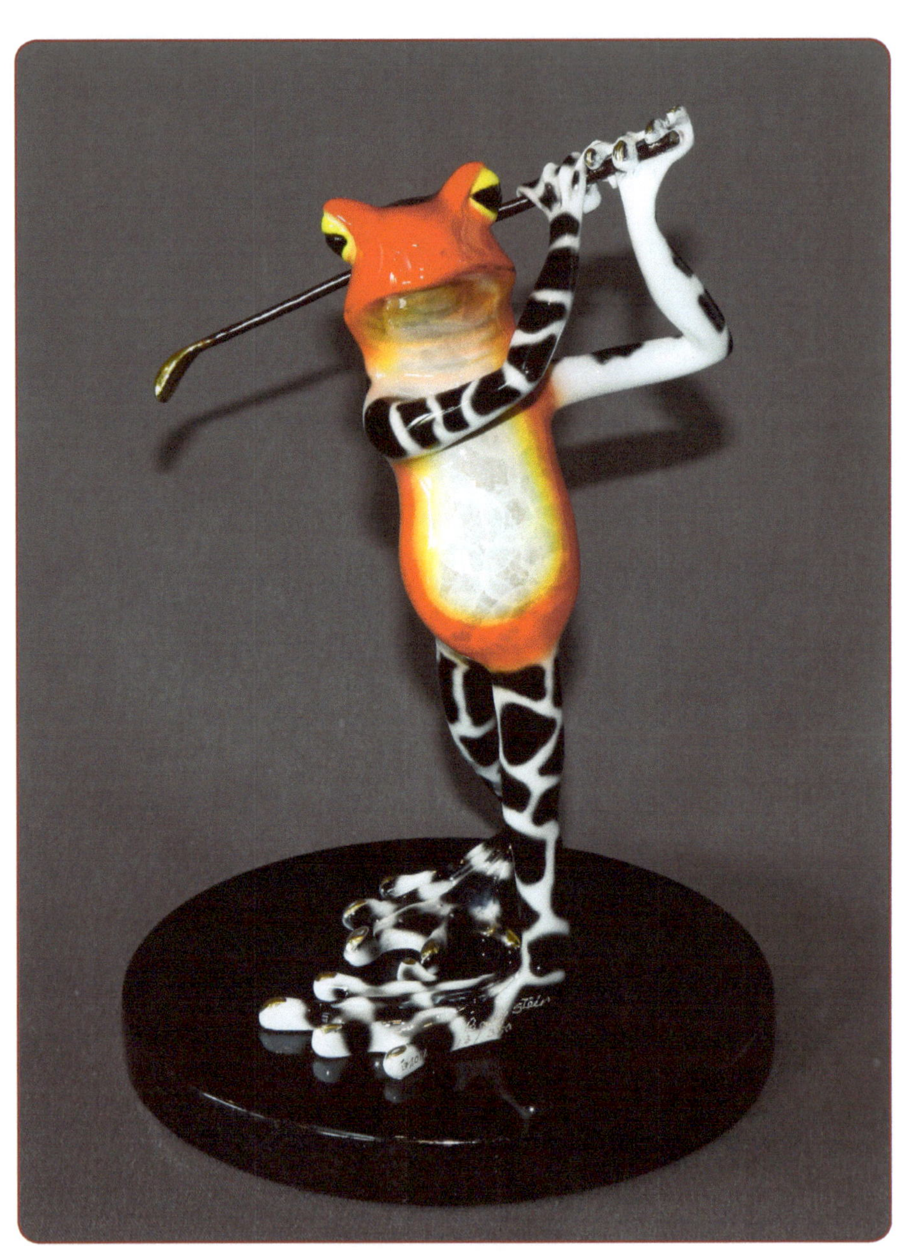

Barry Stein

CHAPTER 6

Frustration

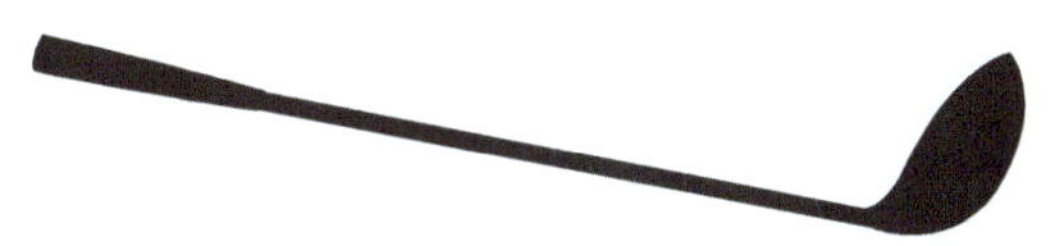

Golf always makes me so damned angry.

KING GEORGE V (1865-1936)

Fuck . . . Shit . . . these are highly difficult golf terms and you're using them on your first lesson—this is promising.

RON SHELTON (b. 1945)

Jimmy Demaret and I had the best sports psychologist in the world. His name was Jack Daniels and he was waiting for us after every round.

JACKIE BURKE (b. 1923)

Swing hard in case you hit it.

DAN MARINO (b. 1961)

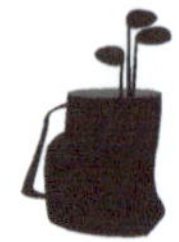

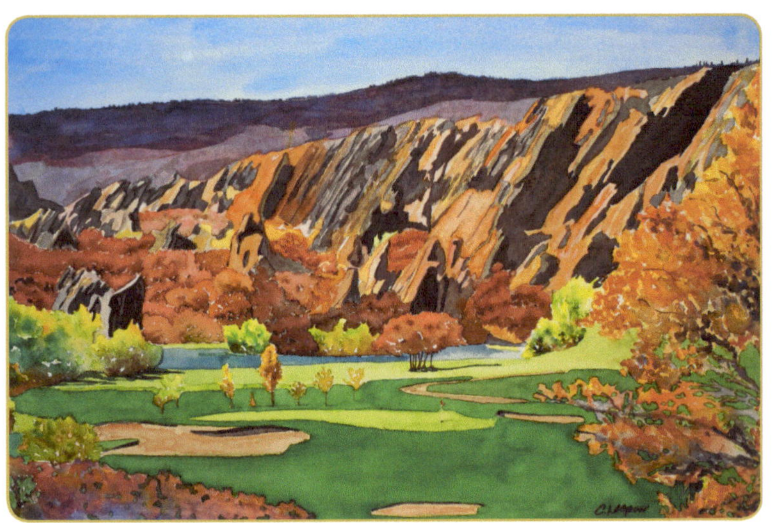

Christine LaGrow

Golfers just love punishment.
And that's where I come in.

PETE DYE (b. 1925)

The trick for the developer, as devised through his architect, is to build something that is photogenically stunning, however impractical, extravagant or absurd. Never mind the golfer, that most gullible of all citizens.

PETER THOMSON (b. 1929)

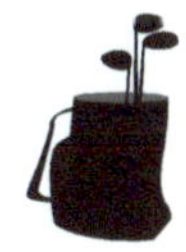

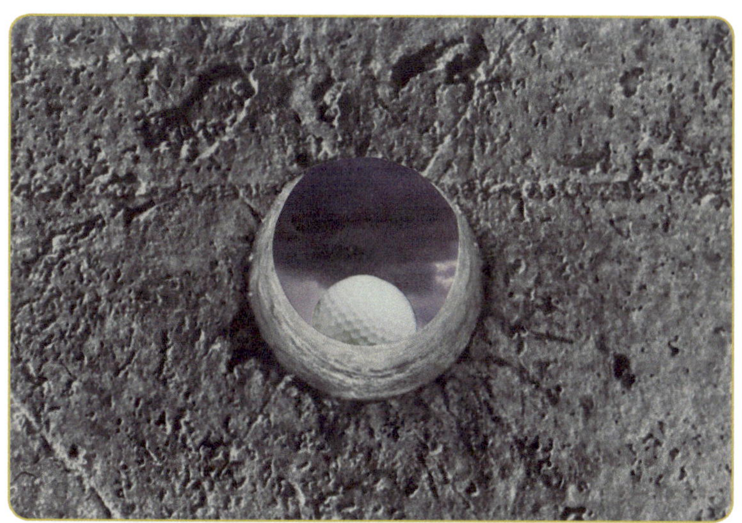

Marian Williams

Ninety percent of putts that are short don't go in.

YOGI BERRA (b. 1925)

I don't have any particular hang-ups about superstitions. I did try them all, but they didn't work.

KATHY WHITWORTH (b. 1939)

If you're stupid enough to whiff, you should be smart enough to forget it.

ARNOLD PALMER (b. 1929)

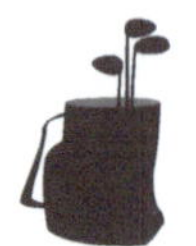

I'm not really interested in sports psychology.
It makes me feel like a crazy person.

MICHELLE WIE (b. 1989)

A million thoughts went through my mind.
What a little mind I have.

FUZZY ZOELLER (b. 1951)

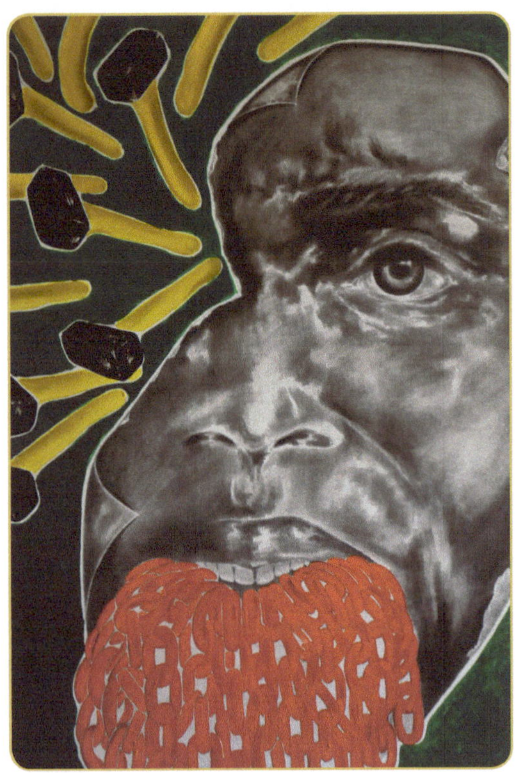

Marlene Jorge

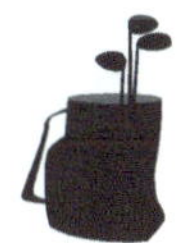

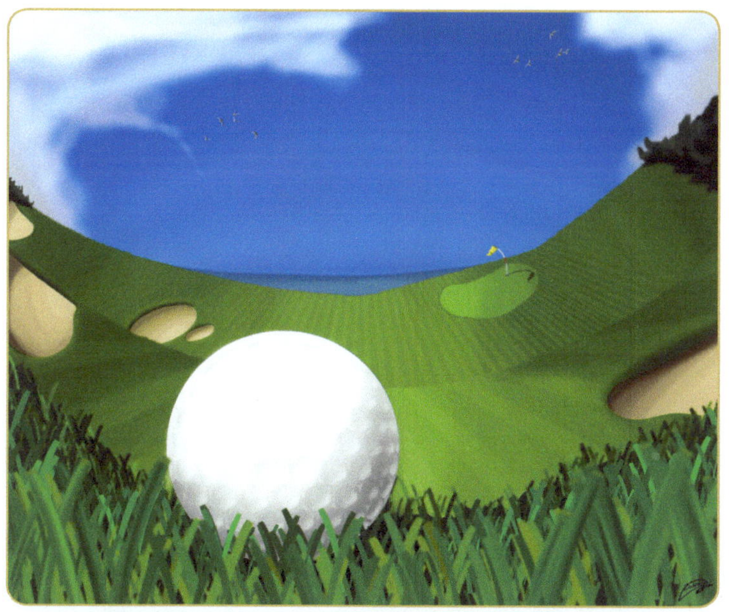

Craig Mann

Of the mental hazards, being scared is the worst.
When you get scared, you get tense.

SAM SNEAD (1912-2002)

In golf, as in no other sport,
your principal opponent is yourself.

HERBERT WARREN WIND (1916-2005)

The clubs were not the problem. My brain was.

PAYNE STEWART (1957-1999)

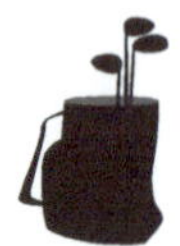

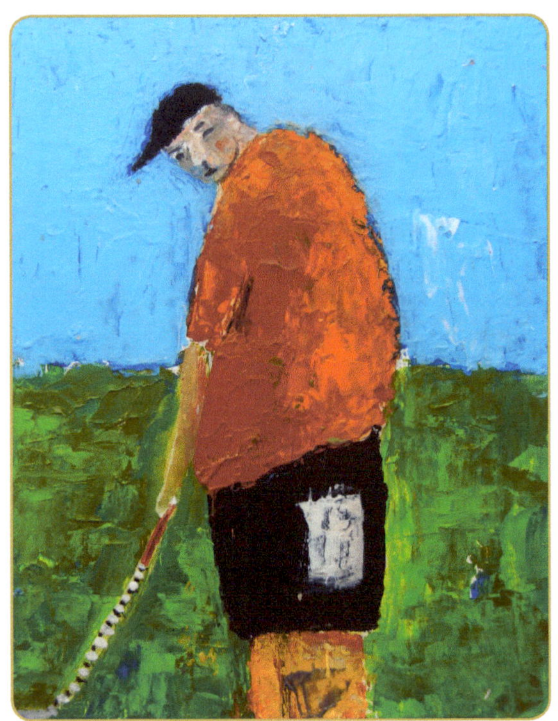

Katherine Wood

I find a better way to let it go. I do something physical to feel better, like slam the club in the rough, slam my bag, or slap a tree.

TOM LEHMAN (b. 1959)

It took me seventeen years to get 3,000 hits in baseball. I did it in one afternoon on the golf course.

HANK AARON (b. 1934)

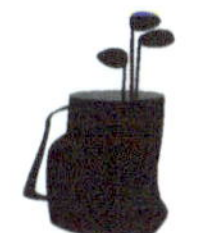

Thinking instead of acting is the number-one golf disease.

SAM SNEAD (1912-2002)

The golf swing is like sex. You can't be thinking about the mechanics of the act while you are performing.

DAVE HILL (1937-2011)

The muttered hint, 'Remember, you have a stroke here,' freezes my joints like a blast from Siberia.

JOHN UPDIKE (1932-2009)

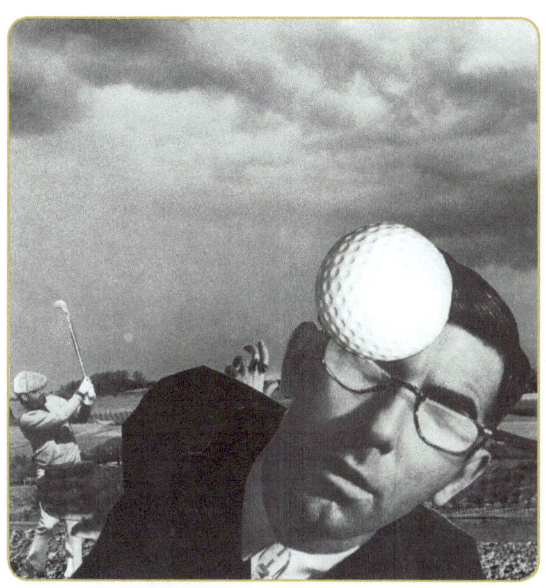

Ben Thompson

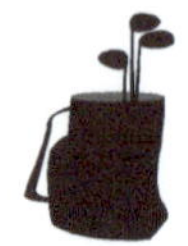

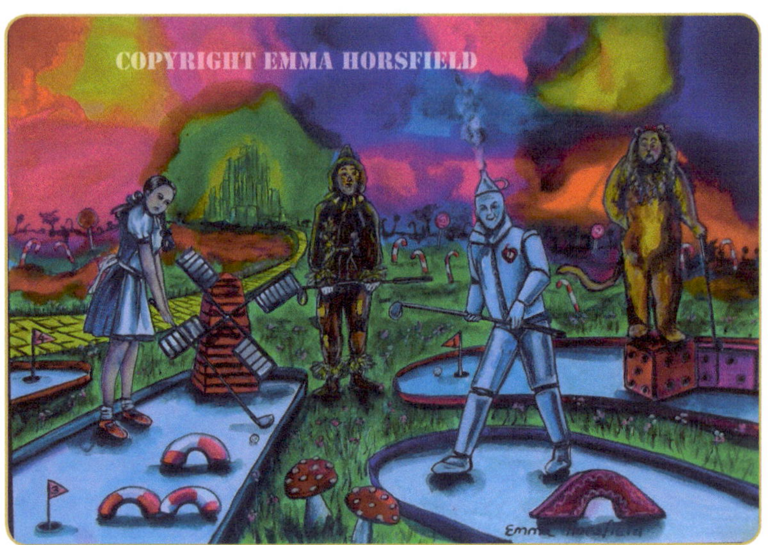

Emma Horsfield

Those who the gods seek to destroy first,
learn how to play golf.

LESLIE NIELSEN (1926-2010)

If you expect a bad lie for even one second,
the gods will know it and give you a bad lie.

MICHELLE WIE (b. 1989)

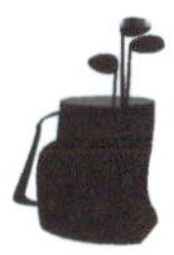

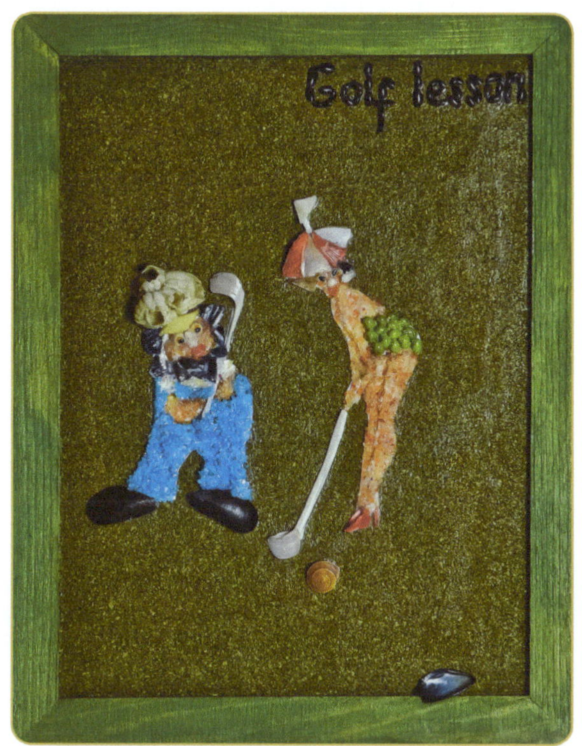

Alla Baksanskaya

The reason the pro tells you to keep your head down is so you can't see him laughing.

PHYLLIS DILLER (1917-2012)

If a lot of people gripped a knife and fork the way they do a golf club, they'd starve to death.

SAM SNEAD (1912-2002)

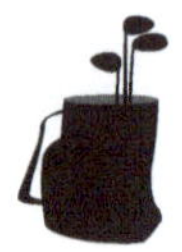

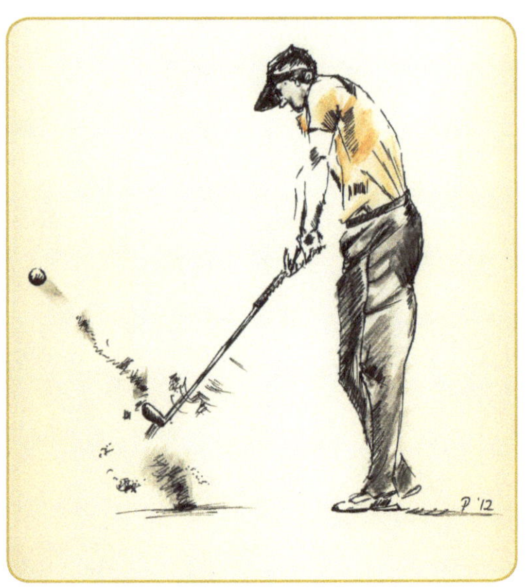

Paulette Farrell

There is no movement in the golf swing so difficult that it cannot be made even more difficult by careful study and diligent practice.

THOMAS BOSWELL (b. 1947)

Too many people carry the last shot with them. It is a heavy and useless burden.

JOHNNY MILLER (b. 1947)

It's a funny thing, the more I practice the luckier get.

GARY PLAYER (b. 1935)

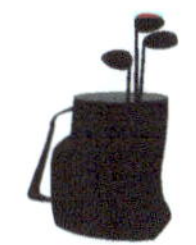

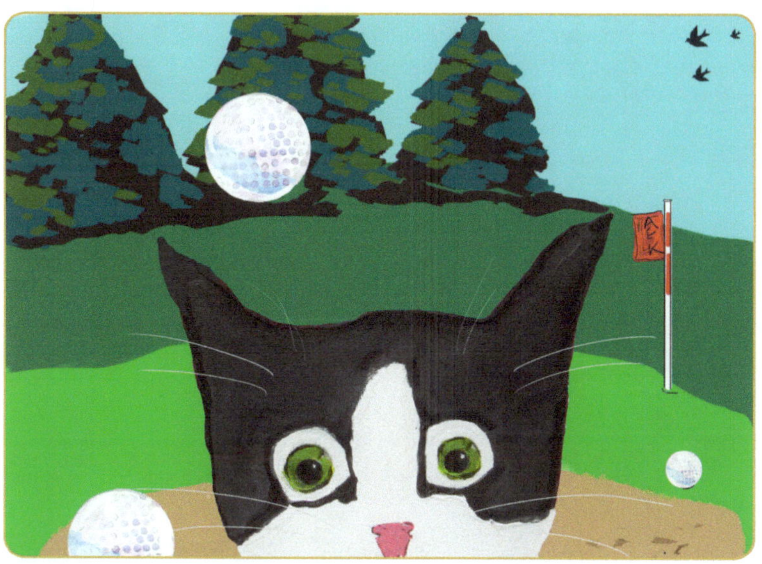

Alison Kurek

Maintain a childhood enthusiasm
for the game of golf.

CHI-CHI RODRIGUEZ (b. 1935)

Golf is deceptively simple and endlessly
complicated; it satisfies the soul and
frustrates the intellect.

ARNOLD PALMER (b. 1929)

Christine LaGrow

CHAPTER 7

Scotland

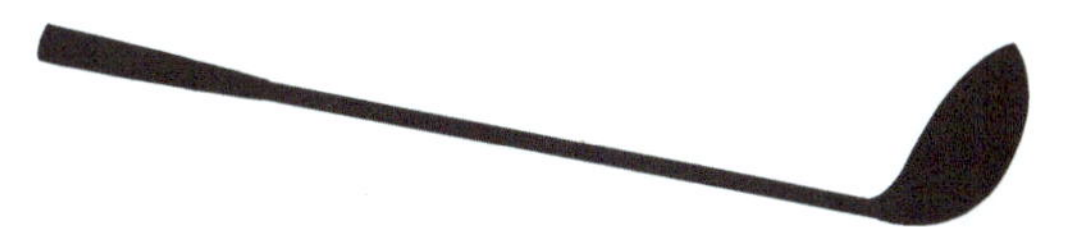

St. Andrews? I feel like I'm back visiting an old grandmother. She's crotchety and eccentric but also elegant. Anyone who doesn't fall in love with her has no imagination.

TONY LEMA (1934-1966)

In so many English sports, something flying or running has to be killed or injured; golf calls for no drop of blood from any living creature.

HENRY LEACH (1923-2011)

It is decreeted and ordained . . . that the Fute-ball and Golfe be utterly cryed downe, and not to be used. And as tuitching the Fute-ball and the Golfe, to be punished by the Barronniss un-law.

JAMES II OF SCOTLAND (1430-1460)

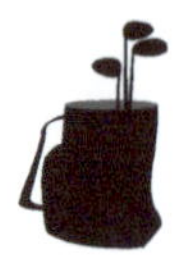

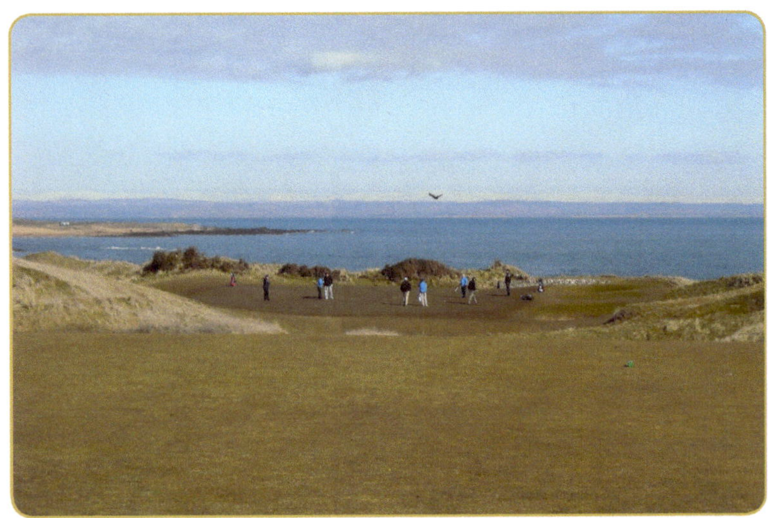

Steve Lamb

Linksland is the old Scottish word for the earth at the edge of the sea . . . You see, the game comes out of the ocean, just like man himself!

MICHAEL BAMBERGER (b. 1960)

Unlike the other Scotch game of whisky-drinking, excess is not injurious to the health.

SIR WALTER SIMPSON (18??-19??)

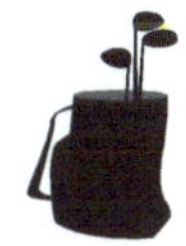

Golf is an exercise which is much used by the Gentlemen of Scotland. A large common in which there are several little holes is chosen for the purpose. It is played with little leather balls stuffed with feathers; and sticks made somewhat in the form of a handy-wicket.

BENJAMIN RUSH (1745-1813)

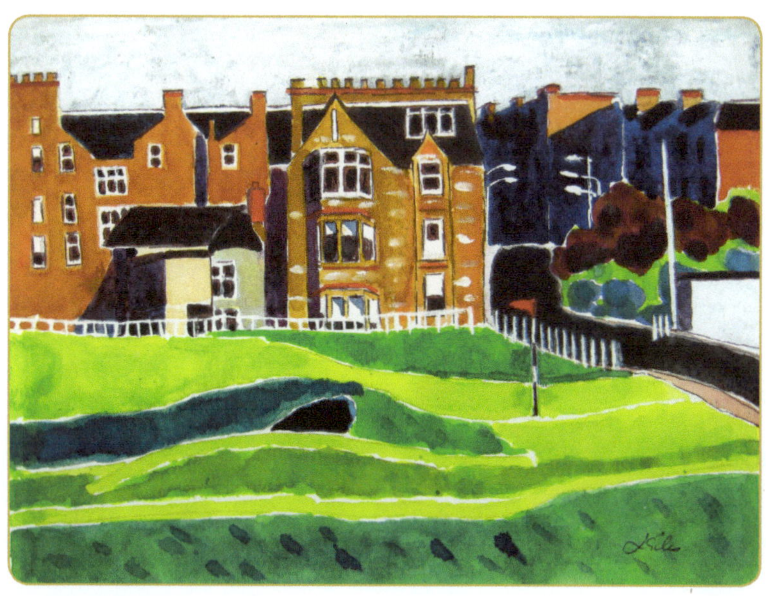

Lesley Giles

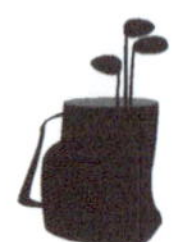

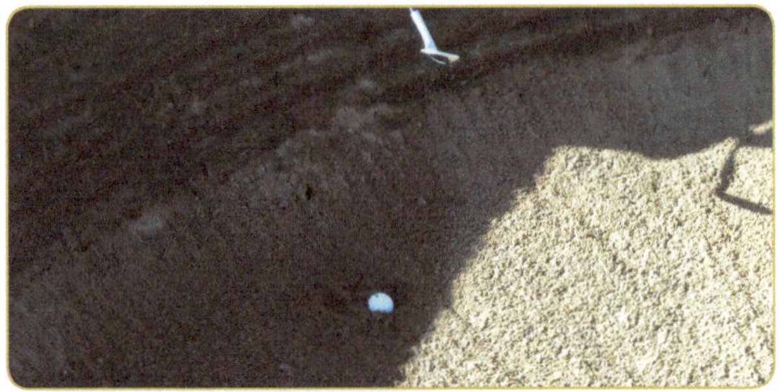

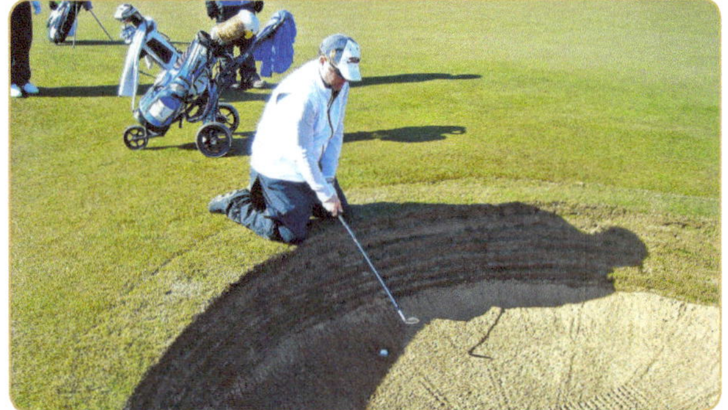

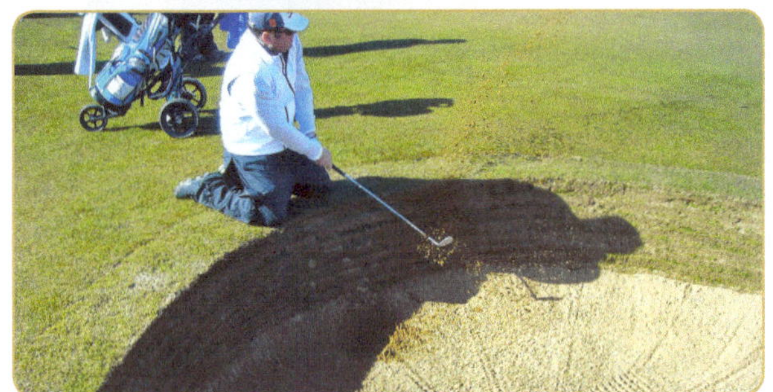

Steve Lamb

YES!

STEVE LAMB (b. 1967)

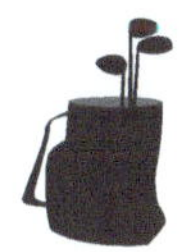

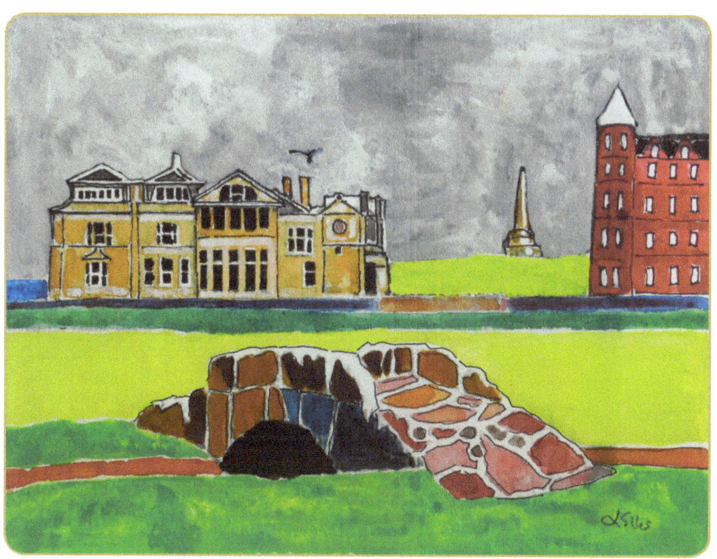

Lesley Giles

Tennis is not in use amongst us, but in lieu of that, you have that excellent recreation of goff-ball than which truly I do not know a better.

THE MARQUIS OF ARGYLL (1607-1661)

King Charles I is said to have been fond of the exercise of the golf. While he was engaged in a party of golf on the Links of Leith, a letter was delivered into his hands, which gave him the first account of the rebellion in Ireland.

WILLIAM TYTLER (1711-1792)

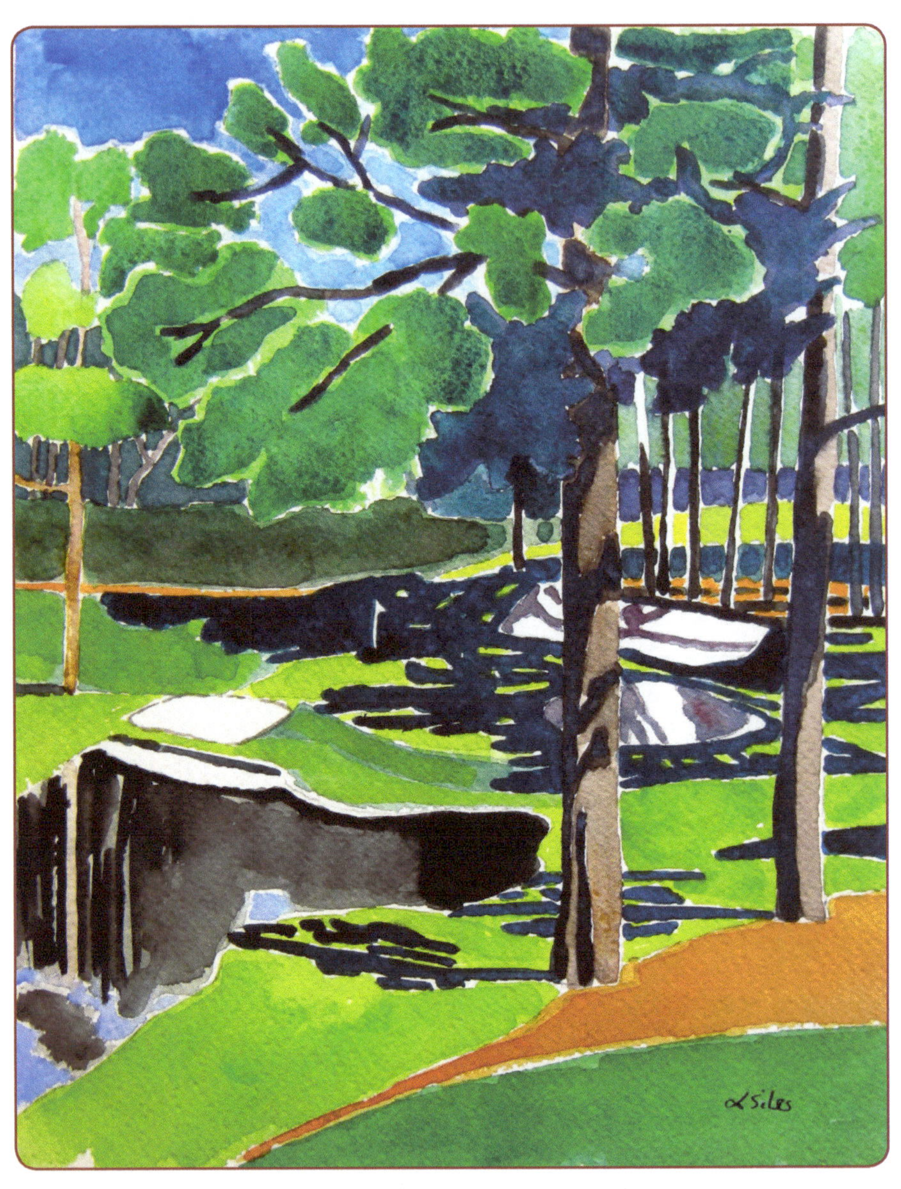

Lesley Giles

CHAPTER 8

Presidential Golf

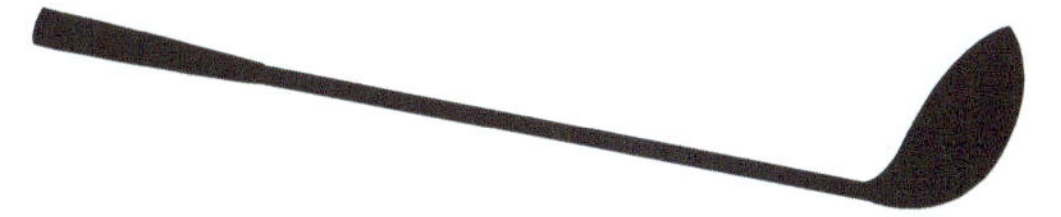

Golf obviously provides one of our best forms of healthful exercise accompanied by good fellowship and companionship.

PRESIDENT DWIGHT D. EISENHOWER (1890-1969)

I know I'm getting better at golf because I'm hitting fewer spectators. Either that, or fewer people are watching me play.

PRESIDENT GERALD FORD (1913-2006)

Golf is a game for people who are not active enough for baseball.

PRESIDENT WILLIAM HOWARD TAFT (1857-1930)

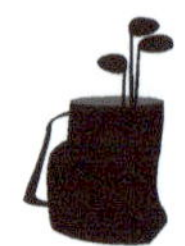

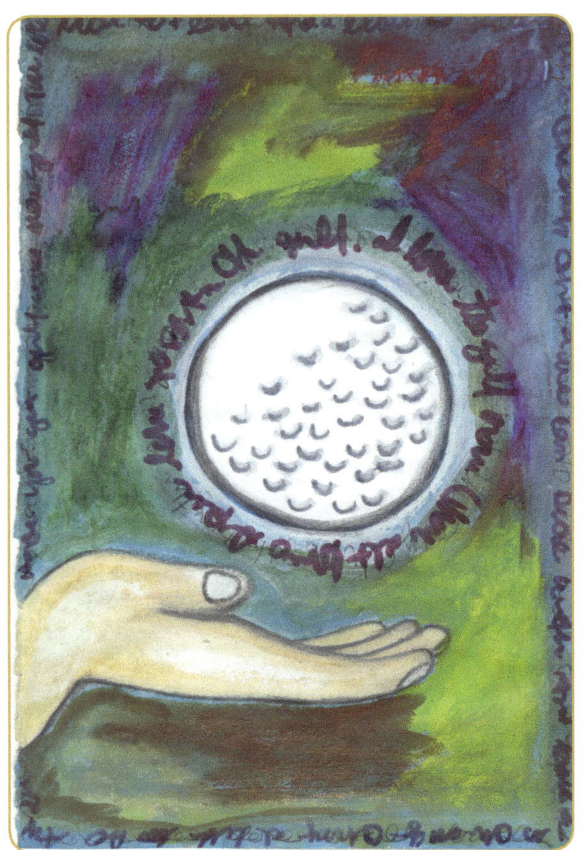

Leslie Rodriguez

"It does look like a very good exercise.
But what is the little white ball for?"
(teasing one of his officers after he swung
and missed the ball completely)

PRESIDENT ULYSSES S. GRANT (1822-1885)

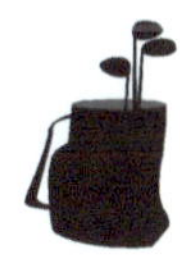

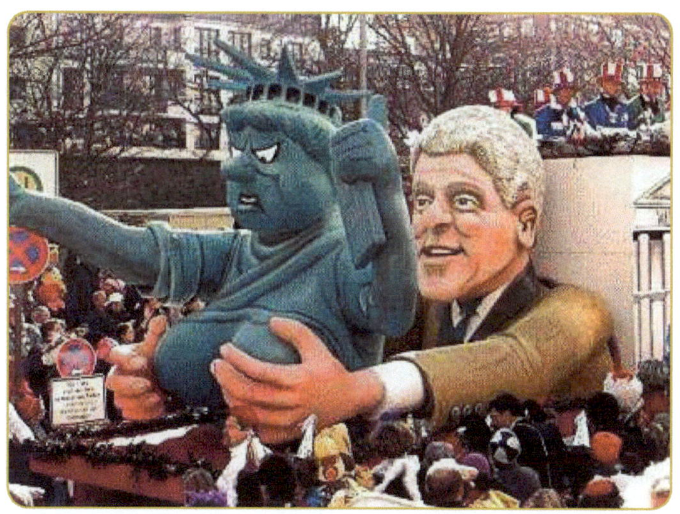

"Rose Monday" Carnival Float

Golf is like life in a lot of ways: The most important competition is the one against yourself. All the biggest wounds are self-inflicted.

PRESIDENT BILL CLINTON (b. 1946)

At the end of the day he (Bill Clinton) had an 82 on his score card, but it took him two hundred swings to get there.

DON VAN NATTA (b. 1964)

If Bill Clinton is an 8-handicap, I'm Bobby Jones.

PRESIDENT GEORGE H. BUSH (b. 1946)

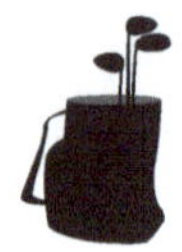

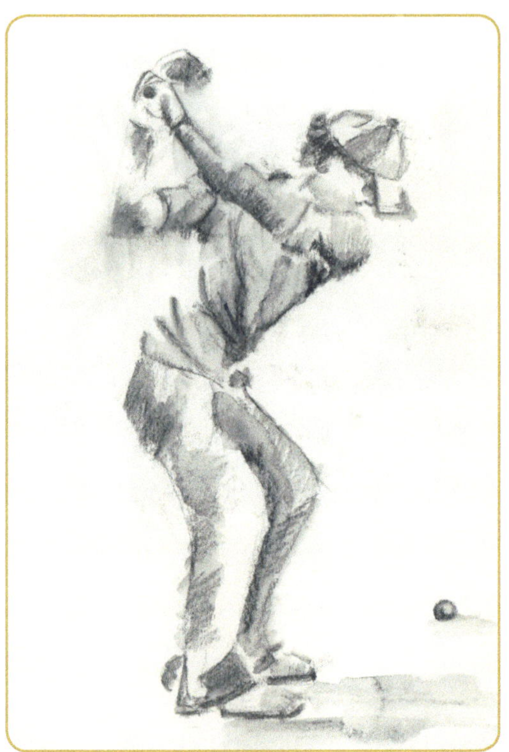

Paulette Farrell

In golf, you keep your head down and follow through. In the vice presidency, you keep your head up and follow through. It's a big difference.

VICE PRESIDENT DAN QUAYLE (b. 1947)

"Dan would rather play golf than have sex any day"

MARILYN QUAYLE (b. 1949)

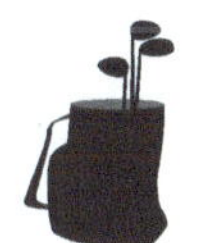

Golf is an ineffectual attempt to put an elusive ball into an obscure hole with implements ill-adapted to the purpose.

PRESIDENT WOODROW WILSON (1858-1924)

Forget that I am president of the United States. I am Warren Harding, playing with some friends, and I'm going to beat the hell out of them.

PRESIDENT WARREN HARDING (1865-1923)

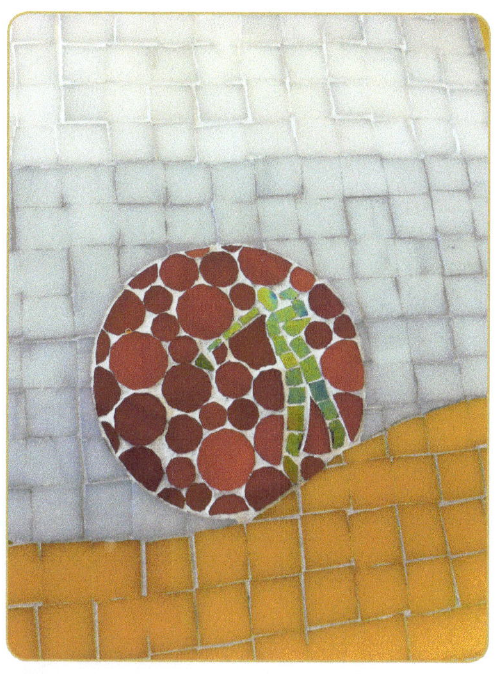

Yalily Mejia

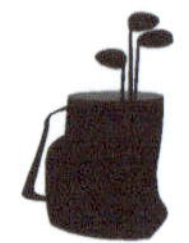

It is true that my predecessor did not object, as I do, to pictures of one's golf skill in action. But neither, on the other hand, did he ever bean a Secret Serviceman.

PRESIDENT JOHN F. KENNEDY (1917-1963)

"My golf-loving friend Bob Hope asked me what my handicap was. So I told him—the Congress."

PRESIDENT RONALD REAGAN (1911-2004)

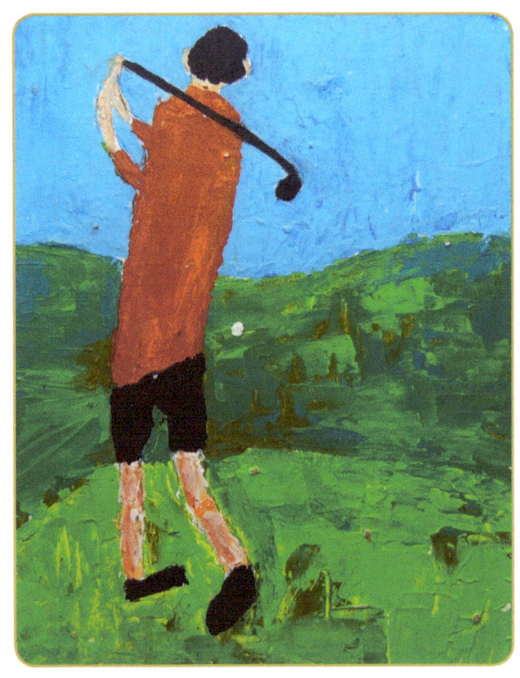

Katherine Wood

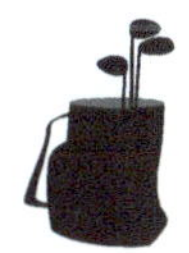

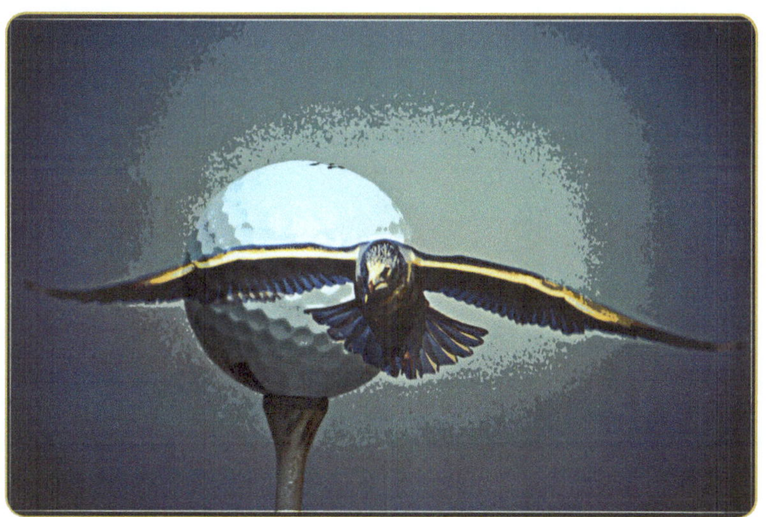

Earl Devendorf

One lesson you better learn if you want to be in politics is that you never go out on a golf course and beat the President.

PRESIDENT LYNDON JOHNSON (1908-1973)

It's amazing how many people beat you at golf now that you're no longer president.

PRESIDENT GEORGE H. BUSH (b. 1946)

President [George H.] Bush does not take mulligans. That family plays by the rules.

BEN CRENSHAW (b. 1952)

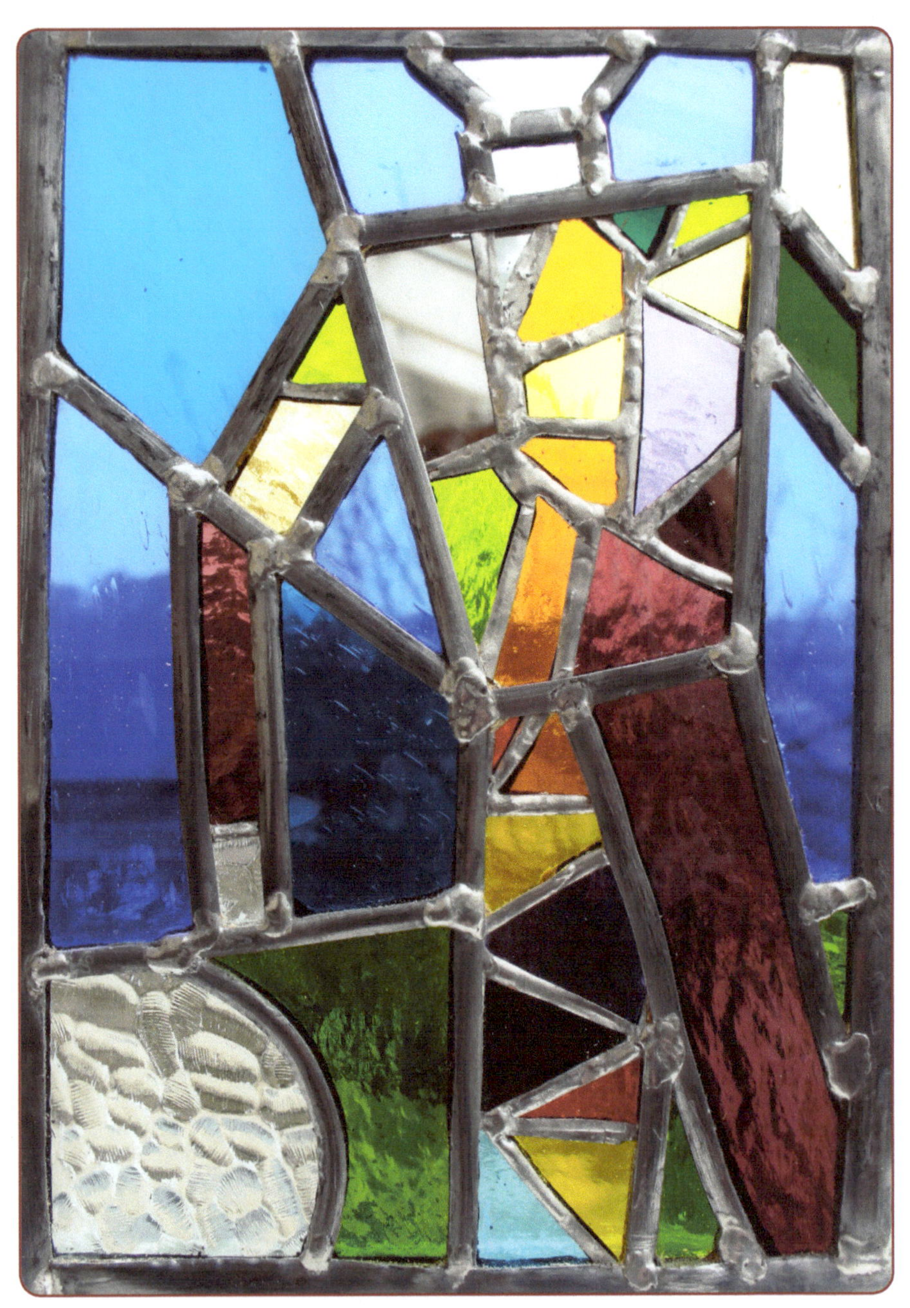

Helen Auburn

CHAPTER 9

Hogan, Jones, Nelson & Snead

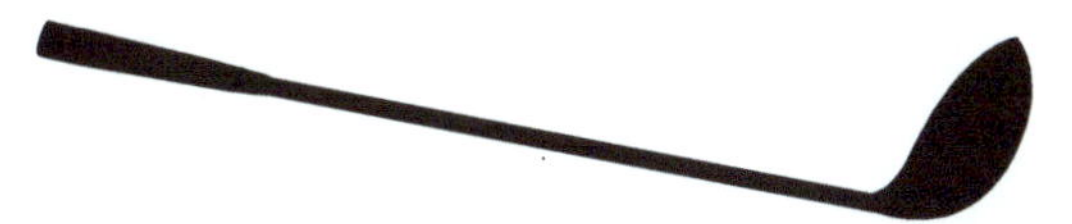

The three things I fear most in golf are lighting, Ben Hogan, and a downhill putt.

SAM SNEAD (1912-2002)

I dreamed I made 17 holes in one, and then on the 18th hole I lipped the cup and I was madder than hell.

BEN HOGAN (1912-1997)

Golf is assuredly a mystifying game. It would seem that if a person has hit a golf ball correctly a thousand times, he should be able to duplicate the performance at will. But this is certainly not the case.

BOBBY JONES (1902-1971)

The only shots you can be sure of are those you've had already.

BYRON NELSON (1912-2006)

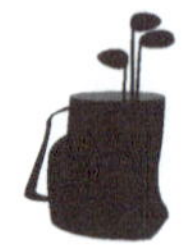

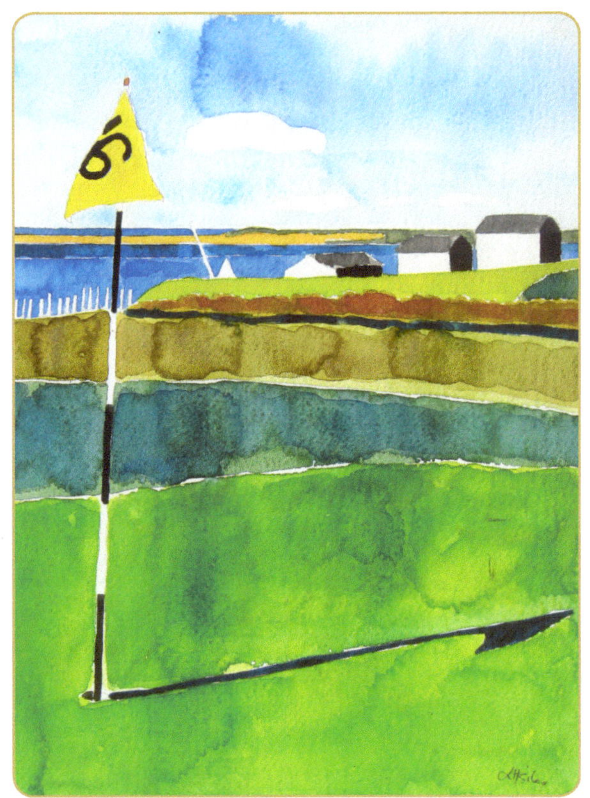

Lesley Giles

I call my sand wedge my 'Half Nelson' because
I can always strangle the opposition with it.

BYRON NELSON (1912-2006)

I play with friends, but we don't play friendly games.

BEN HOGAN (1912-1997)

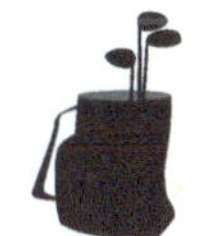

The difference between getting in a sand trap and getting in water is like the difference between an auto wreck and an airplane wreck.

BOBBY JONES (1902-1971)

Too much ambition is a bad thing to have in a bunker.

BOBBY JONES (1902-1971)

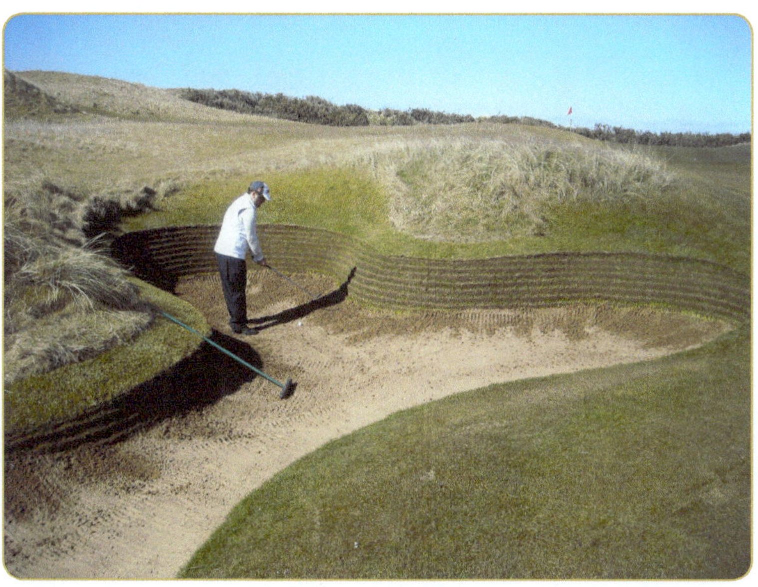

Steve Lamb

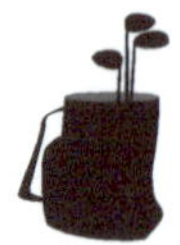

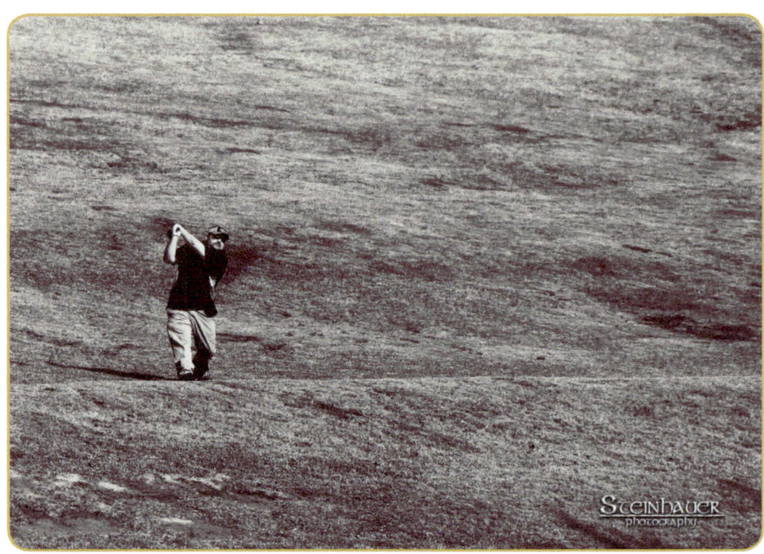

Tony Steinhauer

In those days [the 1930s] the money was
the main thing, the only thing I played for.
Championships were something to grow old with.

BYRON NELSON (1912-2006)

I don't know very much. I know a little bit about
golf. I know how to make a stew.
And I know how to be a decent man.

BYRON NELSON (1912-2006)

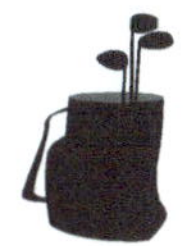

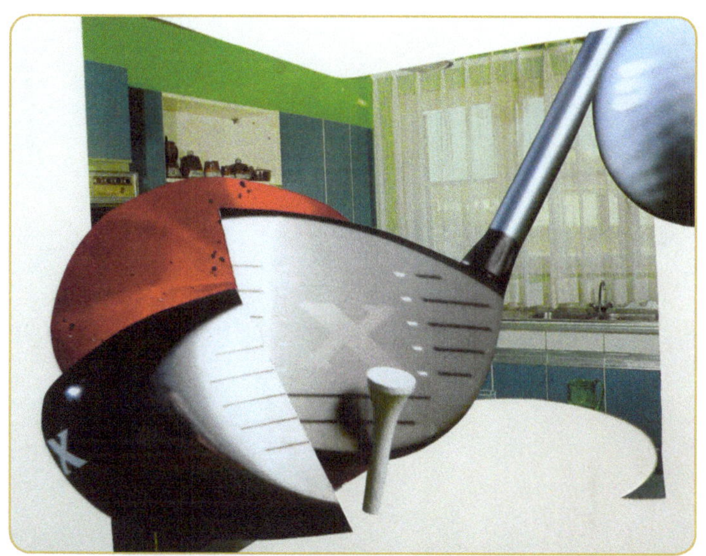

Marian Williams

Golf is not a game of good shots.
It's a game of bad shots.

BEN HOGAN (1912-1997)

Of all the hazards, fear is the worst.

SAM SNEAD (1912-2002)

Golf is a lot like life.
When you make a decision, stick with it.

BYRON NELSON (1912-2006)

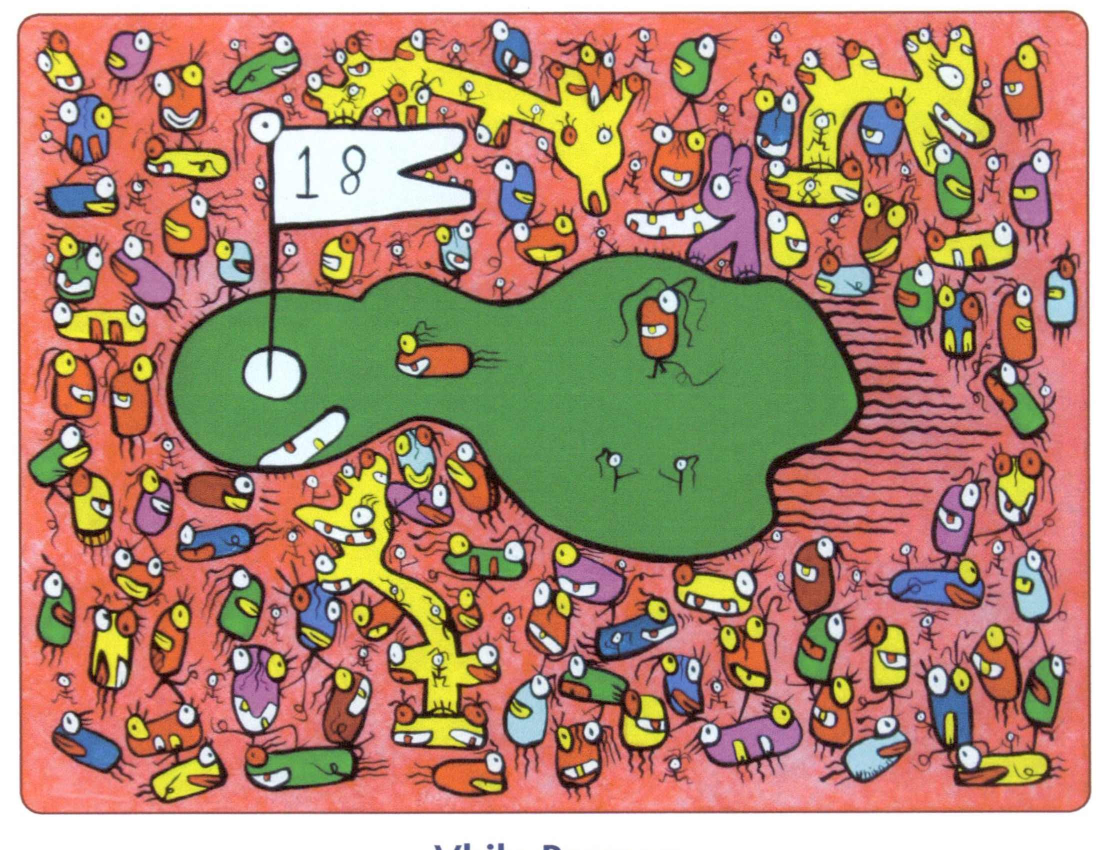

Vhilo Persson

CHAPTER 10

The Back 9

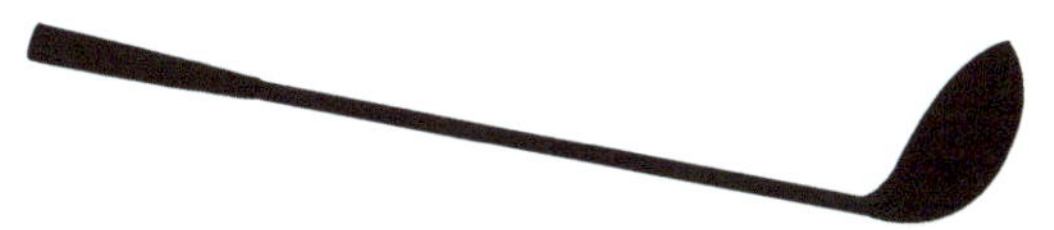

Golf is like love. One day you think you are too old, and the next day you want to do it again.

ROBERTO DE VICENZO (b. 1923)

Anyone who says he plays better at fifty-five than he did at twenty-five wasn't very good at twenty-five.

BOB BRUE (b. 1935)

People have always said, 'Jack, I wish I could play like you.' Well, now they can.

JACK NICKLAUS (b. 1940)

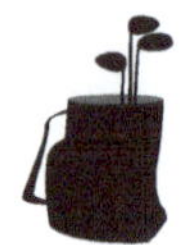

The older I get the better I used to be.

LEE TREVINO (b. 1939)

Everyone used to say to me,
'Glad you won the tournament' . . . and now
they say, 'Glad you made the cut.'

ARNOLD PALMER (b. 1929)

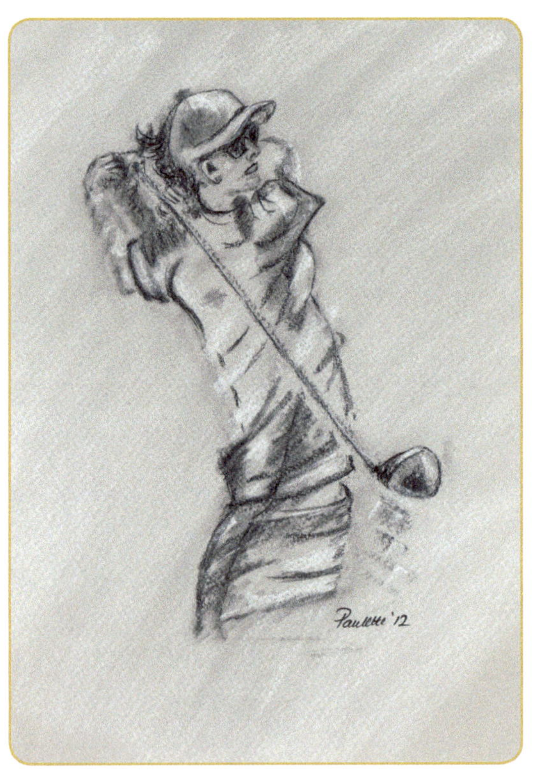

Paulette Farrell

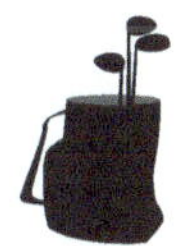

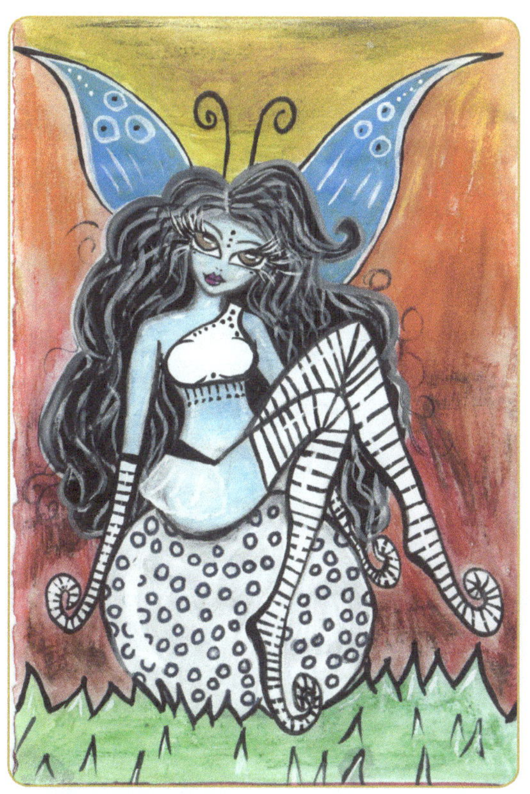

Leslie Rodriguez

The great thing about starting golf in your forties is that you can start golf in your forties. You can start other things in your forties but generally your wife makes you stop them, as Bill Clinton found out.

P.J. O'ROURKE (b. 1947)

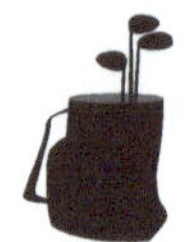

Golf is a lot like sex. Even when you cheat you still have to get it up and in. And that gets tougher and tougher to do every year.

BILLY ORVILE (b. 19??)

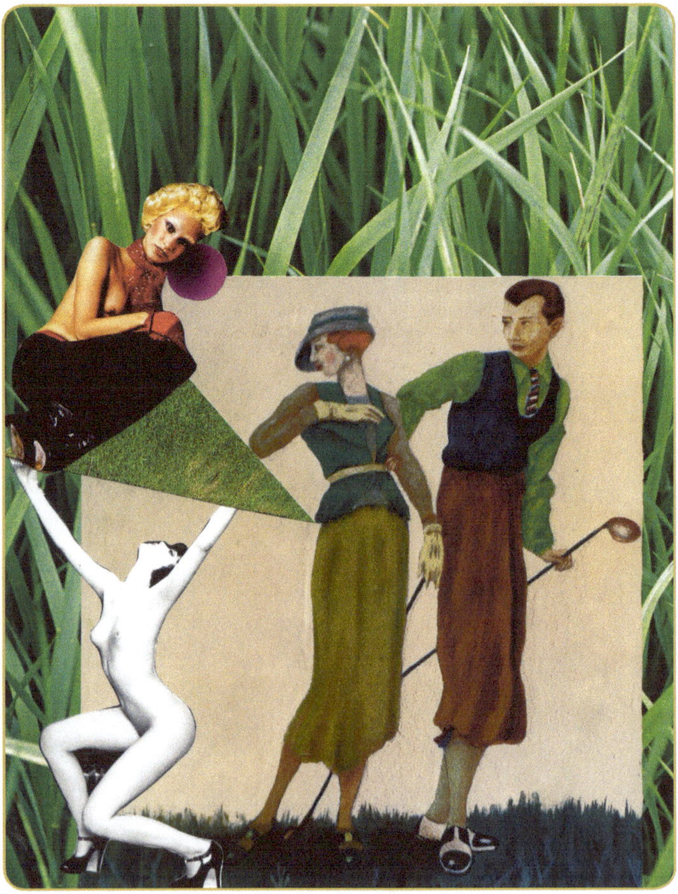

Mongobi-Bibbiana T. Mele

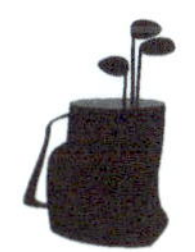

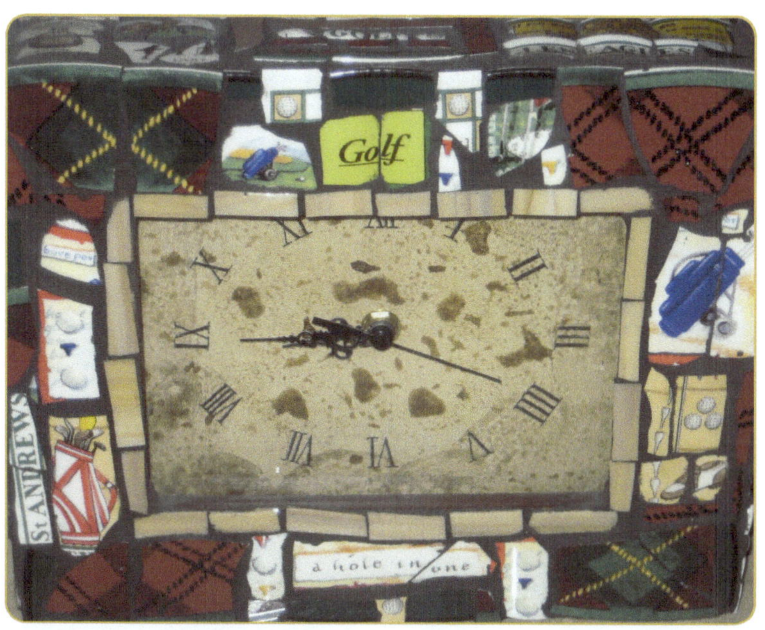

Jackie Spector Linder

I've been playing the game so long that
my handicap is in Roman numerals.

BOB HOPE (1903-2003)

I'm getting so old, I don't even buy
green bananas anymore.

CHI-CHI RODRIGUEZ (b. 1935)

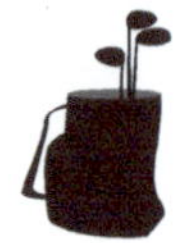

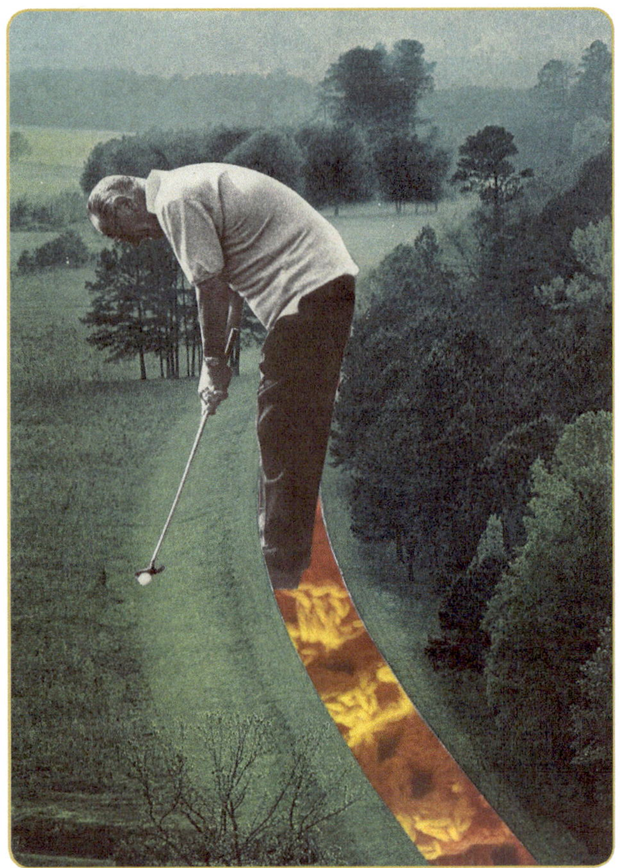

Jesse Treece

One of the nice things about the Senior Tour
is that we can take a cart and cooler. If your game
is not going well, you can always have a picnic.

LEE TREVINO (b. 1939)

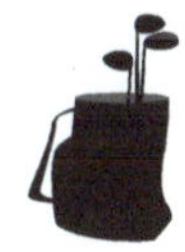

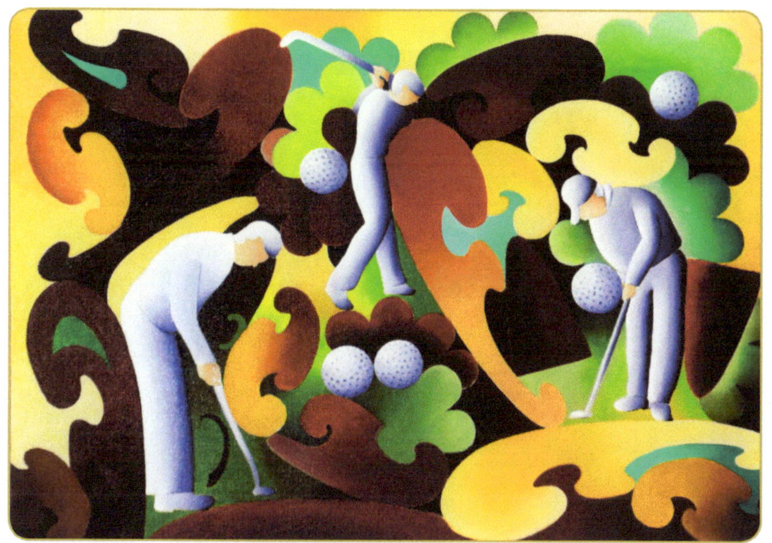

Yvonne Lautenschläger

When you get this old, you wake up with a different pain each day. Besides, it's a grind trying to beat sixty-year-old kids out there.

SAM SNEAD (1912-2002)

You know you're getting old when all the names in your black book have 'M.D.' after them.

ARNOLD PALMER (b. 1929)

Coombies Voted 2013 BECK'S OPEN Sex Symbol

Damn I love a
Golfer with a stiff shaft

Coombsie I am
Exercising my
Breasts for you.

Look at his
Tight ASS

Why is he in love
With Pharadey
When I am so HOT

Those boots get the
Women every
Time.

I wonder what he
Looks like Naked.

He still can't mow the
Lawn worth shit.

I'm wet

oombsie you
Are my God.

Dave, I know you
Love your women
Flexible !

Prouts Neck Maine 2013

Charles Andrews

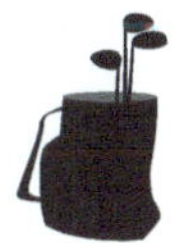

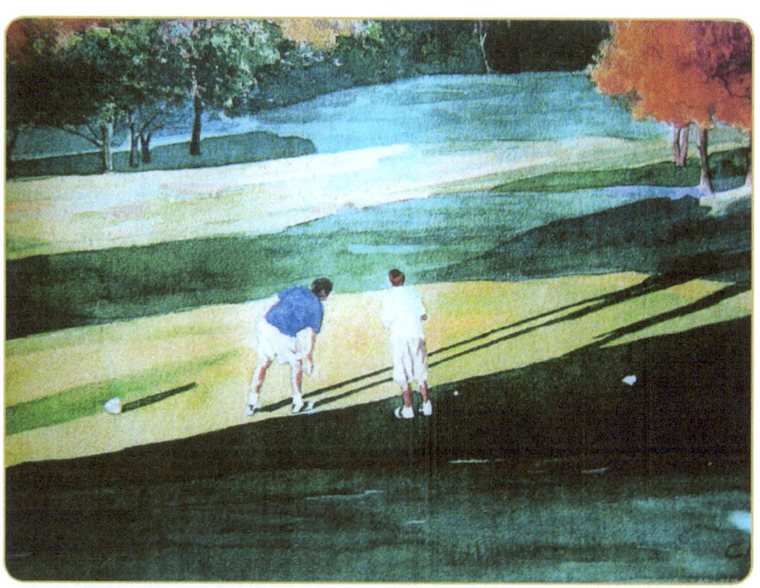

Christine LaGrow

Then I was skinnier, I hit it better.
I putted better and I could see better.
Other than that, everything's the same.
HOMERO BLANCAS (b. 1938)

It's a lot nicer looking down on the grass
instead of looking up at it.
ARNOLD PALMER (b. 1929)

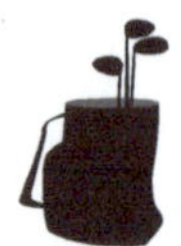

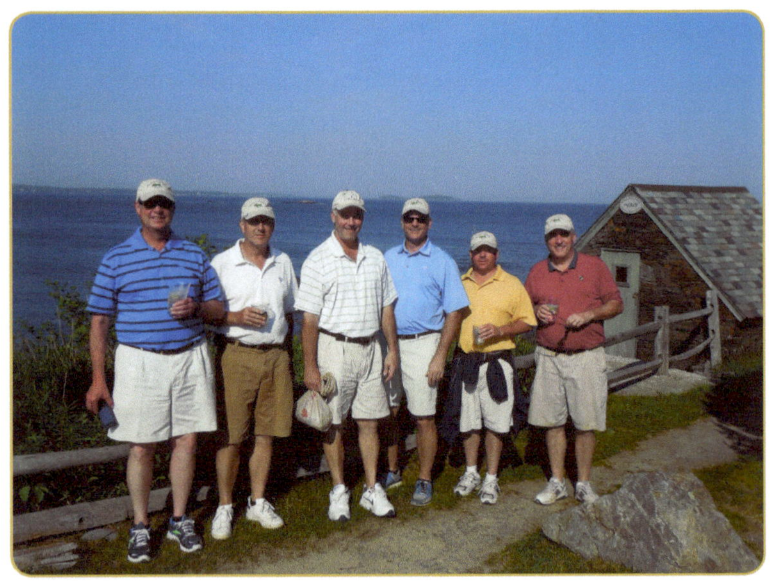

Charles Andrews

It's a little like sex. One bad performance and you begin to wonder.

JULIUS BOROS (1920-1994)

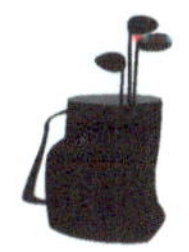

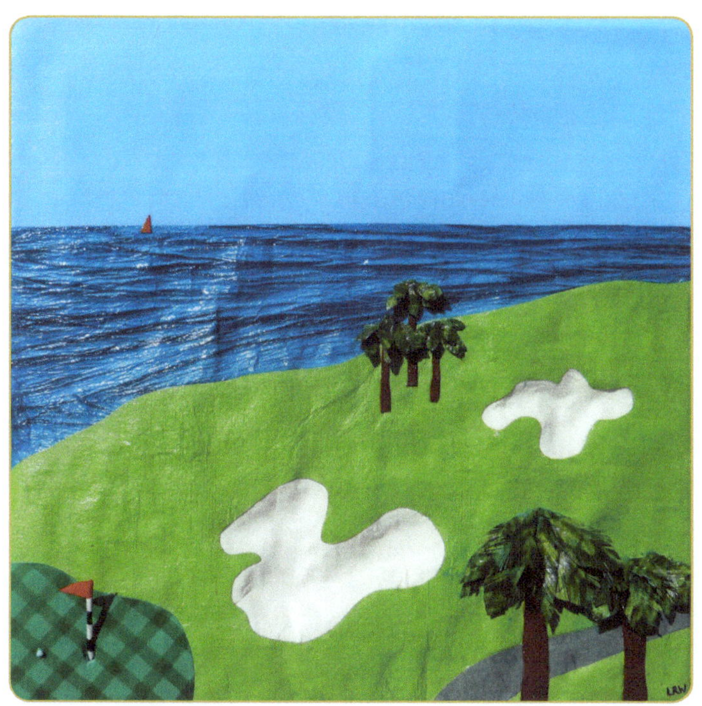

Laurel Woolstenhulme

Retire to what? I already play golf and fish for a living.

JULIUS BOROS (1920-1994)

That's life. The older you get, the tougher it is to score.

BOB HOPE (1903-2003)

Don't ever get old.

BEN HOGAN (1912-1997)

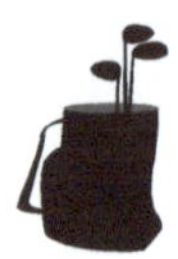

Artists & Photographers Biographies

Charles Andrews III—Page 35, 37, 46, 92, 94

Charles Andrews III is a multifaceted artist who exhibits in many outdoor settings. His large paint on wood sculptures are known for the social and political statements they make. The controversial nature and location of some of his exhibits has caused local authorities to become involved.

Charles's studio, located south of Cazenovia, NY in Pig City, is open to visitors by appointment. For commission work contact him through facebook or by phone at 315 727 5370.

Helen Auburn—Page 78

Helen Auburn graduated from the University of Sunderland in June 2011. She has a BA Honors in Glass and Ceramic art. She spent her second year on exchange at San Jose State University, California.

She welcomes commissions. "Glass as a medium excites me, with the depth of color, versatility and light emitting qualities that it allows. I have a fascination with tactility. My work encompasses texture that produces within the viewer a desire to touch. Color is key. Pattern and repetition are important concepts and the more excessive something is, the better it is. To educate myself further about the world and art are my two main goals in life. Traveling is a crucial element of being for me, to engage socially with others and experience the world not only enriches my mind but also greatly influences my work."

For more information on her work website address is

http://helenauburn.wix.com/helenauburnglass

helenauburn@hotmail.co.uk

Mobile: +44 756 308 6128 or visit her facebook page Helen Auburn Glass Artist.

Alla Baksanskaya—Page 22, 47, 61

Alla Baksanskaya is a award winning artist working with natural seashells. She uses colorful seashells and acrylic paint to create her unique three-dimensional works of art. She creates mosaic, collages, figurines and other

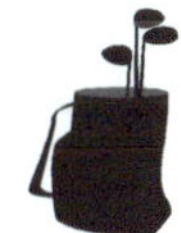

decorative items. All of those are unique, one of a kind items. Alla's style is modern, from abstract flowers to portraits, from mosaics to acrylic or oil paintings and from diptychs to art collages.

Alla won numerous awards at prestigious Sanibel Island, FL and Philadelphia seashell shows in 2009 and 2010.

Since 1994 Alla has lived in New York City with her family. It is here where she has started to create art full time.

Visit her website www.allaexpression.com or on facebook at Alla Baksanskaya

Lauren Brenner—Page 12

Lauren S. Brenner is a self-taught collage artist and professional writer from Southern California. She began collaging in the '70s as a teenager under the influence of Pop Tarts, pop art, Eastern philosophy, and a 12-year sentence to Los Angeles public schools. Decades later, she still creates with paper, scissors, and glue, and makes no apologies for folding, spindling, and mutilating any and all forms of printed matter. She uses hand-cut images, words, discarded objects, random ephemera, and acrylic paint to create her surreal worlds and provocative themes on canvas and home furnishings.

Website: www.OpenArted.com, Email: OpenArted@me.com
Facebook: Collage Art By Lauren Brenner

Drace Brown—Page 20

Drace Brown of dRaCeFaCe Imagers has been a portrait artist for 16 years and has professionally created pieces for 6 yrs. Starting at a very young age recreating images of animated characters, Drace began her journey of art moving onward to comics, anime, then studying the great masters of the Renaissance. From there she gained a great love of the human body and its function during motions and emotions.

Drace now works with a team of models, photographers, makeup artists, and hairstylists to create a shoot of the image she has in mind or an incredible idea the model suggested and wanted to come true. She is skilled in oil painting, pastel, chalk, and pencil but, predominately works with Ball Point Ink pens to create life-like images. Drace loves working with people and hearing ideas, so she always anxious to work along with those who want to create artistically a new idea. You can view hour work at: www.facebook.com/draceface. Drace's email is: brown.drace@gmail.com

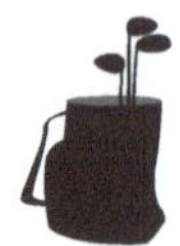

Paul Buford—Page 40

Paul Buford is an artist living in Brandon, MS. He was first introduced to watercolor during his studies at the Mississippi State University School of Architecture. Paul is a licensed architect by trade, but has a great passion for art. He finds beauty in the mystery wrapped in decayed, antique, worn items and seeks to explore those hidden stories through many of his works. Paul always welcomes questions regarding commissions, and he can be contacted at paul@pebarts.com. You can learn more about Paul from his website www.pebarts.com and find him on facebook at Paul Buford.

Sheila Delgado—Page 38

Sheila Delgado studied graphic design and computer graphic arts, but is mainly a self taught artist. While watercolor is often her first choice, she works equally in acrylic, mixed media, digital art, fabric and surface design. She finds inspiration in the Southern California landscape, from the flourishing coast, to the barren high desert.

You are welcome to contact her at shemar67@gmail.com. To view more of her work: https://www.facebook.com/sheila.delgado.10

Spoonflower: http://www.spoonflower.com/profiles/demouse

Earl Devendorf—Page 43, 49, 77

Earl Devendorf is a professional photographer from Carbondale PA. He enjoys photographing a wide range of subjects.

View his work on facebook at: https://www.facebook.com/earl.devendorf or contact him at: earldevendorf@yahoo.com

Paulette Farrell—Page 13, 62, 74, 86

Contact Paulette about her work at pauletteafarrell@hotmail.com

Lior Immanuel Fischer—Page 36

Lior was born in Bern Switzerland and developed an interest in art at an early age. He enjoys producing artwork that explores the psychological effect colors can have on the human mind and mood. See more of Lior's work at www.modernartist.webs.com or visit him on facebook at www.facebook.com/lior.fischer

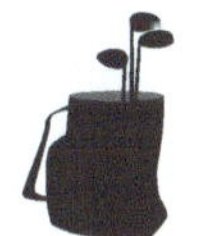

Lezlie Foster—Page 48

Lezlie Foster lives on the Grand Mesa in Western Colorado. She is an amateur photographer, as well as, working with hot glass and she loves to combine the two. She works in soft glass creating beads which she incorporates into one of a kind pieces of jewelry and other unique items. She loves the outdoors and the beautiful forests which she lives in. In her leisure time she rides her mule, fishs, boats, ATVs and hikes.

She can be reached at creekbottomglass@gmail.com. Visit her website http://www.creekbottomglass.com/ or on Facebook at Creek Bottom Glass—Lezlie Foster, Artist

Lesley Giles—Page 6, 10, 16, 24, 25, 26, 50, 67, 69, 70, 80

Lesley Giles is an internationally collected artist from England. She lived & painted in London most of her life until, she moved to Florida in 2003 with her American husband to follow his career. They re-located to the Eastern Shore, Md in 2012 where she paints in her studio overlooking the wild Choptank River.

Lesley is primarily a landscape painter inspired by solitary places and isolated objects which, was why her husband (an avid golfer) could see a potential for her to paint GOLF COURSES—very strange landscapes! She paints with oil, watercolor & pastel; vital to her work is a strong & theatrical light. In 1999 she was selected to be the **Tournament Artist** for the **Ladies European Tour** which involved traveling with the tour & exhibiting her paintings at different club houses along with painting commissions that were used as tournament prizes. The most memorable tournaments were the *Laura Davies Invitational* at Brocket Hall, **England**, the *Rover European Cup* at Praia D'El Rey, **Portugal**, which pitted the Men's European Seniors v the Ladies & the very evocative Marrakech Palmeraie Open in **Morocco.**

"My golf paintings are somewhat different from the more usual 'photographic-type' paintings but they have proved to be immensely popular. In fact, I have just completed a commission ***Dusk at Harbour Town, South Carolina,*** *for a golfer living in Texas. The original was sold a couple of years ago & he loved the painting so much that he commissioned a second version".*

Aside from tournaments Lesley has also visited & painted numerous golf courses in the UK & the USA as well as painting some of the most famous players. She has walked "inside the ropes" with some of the top players including Tiger Woods.

Lesley is a graduate of **Goldsmiths' College**, BFA, and the **Royal College of Art**, MFA, London. She has exhibited extensively in galleries and museums in the UK, Europe, the USA and also, in China following a Visiting Painter invitation to Urumqi, Xinjiang in 1996. Lesley has had solo shows in London, Florida, France and China. Her work has been published by Harper Collins in "Watercolour Masterclass" and "The Challenge of Landscape" as well as being featured in several magazines.

Her paintings are collected all over the world & they can be found in private and museum collections in the United Kingdom, the United States, France, China & Australia.

"... The boldness of her colour is matched by a strength of design that is all too rare in contemporary art. Here is an artist with a down-to-earth sureness of vision that is immensely beguiling"—**Andrew Lambirth**, Art Writer, Spectator Magazine, London, 2006

Lesley's website www.lesleygilesart.com

Email: lesleygilesart@aol.com

Facebook Page: lesley.giles.12@facebook.com

Gene Gissin—Page 44

Gene Gissin is a graduate of RIT College of Graphic Arts and Photography. He owns Gene Gissin Photography where he specializes in photographing everything from weddings to pets. Further, Gissin also works in photojournalism and has taught photography at Cazenovia College in Cazenovia, New York. He is the former President of the Professional Photographers Society of Central New York and the Greater Cazenovia Area Chamber of Commerce. For more of Gissin's work, visit his website at www.gissinphoto.com

Jesse Glenn—Page 19

Jesse Glenn has had a passion for creating art her entire life. She was born in Kentucky and has lived in the city of Berea since the age of thirteen. She studied art and graphic design at Spencerian College in Lexington, KY. Her paintings have been featured in numerous art shows and exhibitions throughout the years.

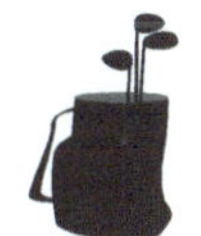

She works mostly with acrylics on canvas and digital media although sometimes she likes to use good old ink and paper.

In some of her work she uses bright, vivid colors, in others she uses high contrast black and white.

Visit Jesse's website at: www.jglennmodernart.com or on facebook at www.facebook.com/jglennmodernart

Shawn Marie Hardy—Page 8, 34

Collage-a-Dada is a project born in the imagination of mixed-media artist, Shawn Marie Hardy. Shawn Marie dissects long forgotten pages from antique and mid-century books and magazines, and re-assemble the contents to create montages reminiscent of old "B" movie stills. The real and logical are reanimated into something more tantalizing and sometimes disturbing. This blend of random images and spontaneous placement is a marriage that combines beauty, ugliness, humor, and disquiet. The result is a portfolio of images that invites the viewer on a phantasmic journey to where the macabre and vagary are commonplace.

Shawn Marie has been a lifelong artist and has exhibited her work in the U.S. and New Zealand.

Visit her websites at: www.collageadada.com and www.shawnmhardy.com or on facebook at: www.facebook.com/collageadada

Emma Horsfield—Page 60

Emma Horsfield is an independent Artist and Illustrator working in oils, pastels, acrylics and inks, whose style is unique and recognizable, with strong contrast and color. All her original art comes straight from the imagination and although she paints mainly fantasy art she also takes portrait commissions which she paints in a realistic style. She has painted portraits for clients in the U.K, U.S.A, and Switzerland, and sold her fantasy art worldwide. She has won many competitions for her artwork. While raising a large family has succeeded in becoming a sought after artist and illustrator. Emma is also planning a book with her own illustrations to be released within the next two years.

Emma Horsfield can be contacted on one of her websites:

www.emmahorsfield.com and www.emmahorsfield.co.uk or on facebook at Artist Illustrator Emma Horsfield

Email: emmahorsfieldart@gmail.com

Marlene Jorge—Page 31, 56

Marlene Jorge's art display a complex set of influences from her rich and varied life. Born in the Dominican Republic, Marlene's art reflexes her Caribbean inheritance with bold colors, stylized posses, echoes of the warm, and tropical surroundings where the artist grew up. Intensely melancholic gazes and movement are essential elements to her oeuvre, as, too, is the gentle dominance of the human figure expressed in a nostalgic manner. One of the recurring features Marlene's artwork posseses is the accentuation of the figure through blank outlines in each on of her pieces dramatizing it in a illustrative way.

Marlene has exhibited in over 30 art shows and galleries around the world. The artist now divides her time between New York and Austin,TX.

Visit her website at www.marlenejorge.com or contact her by phone at 512.560.3144 or by email at Artistmarjorge@gmail.com

Alison Kurek—Page 63

Alison Kurek works are based on sketches and over-active imagination. Her work tends to be on the happy side. Alison says "There is too much stress in our day to day lives; I want my work to make people laugh. My subject matter includes animals and human figures and, recently taken an interest in art history and iconic cultural references." She is a graduate of the State University of New York College at Buffalo where she studied fine art, graphic design and business. Alison also studied at the University of Buffalo and Visual Studies Workshop. She has sold her work through shops, galleries, and art festivals since the 1990s and, has recently expanded her reach by selling through the internet. Alison's work is held in private collections throughout the United States, Canada, Europe, Asia, the Middle East and Australia.

View her works or contact her at the following websites:
Web Store: http://SilentMyloStudio.etsy.com
Facebook: https://www.facebook.com/ArtistAlisonEKurek
Facebook: https://www.facebook.com/SilentMyloTuxedoCat
Blog: www.alisonekurek.com

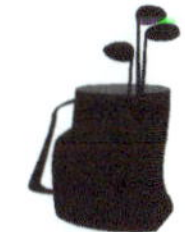

Christine LaGrow—Page 27, 54, 64, 93

Christine currently lives and paints in Chico, California. Her roots are from Southern California, where she attended San Diego State University and studied Arts and Business.

Since 1973, she and her husband moved north to be near Lake Tahoe and the Napa Valley wine country. This has been the inspiration for the Oils and Watercolor paintings she has created over the last thirty years.

In 1998, American Golf Company signed a contract with Christine to exclusively paint watercolors of "Golf Art" for the club and the members. Her work is displayed at the club and at pro golf shops in the area. Sierra Sunrise Gallery has carried and displayed her work for many years.

Christine is one of just a few artists who paint in the wine country areas of Napa and Sonoma. Her watercolors and oils depict the off the path aura of the valley and the beauty of the wine region. The Lake Tahoe art is inspired by the height and depth of the colors of God's most spectacular creation.

Christine will paint custom paintings for personal or business. She creates new original paintings of people and places from your photos.

Please visit her collection displayed at ART.COM, FaceBook page at "Inspirational art by Christine LaGrow" or her website at

www.christinelagrowgallery.com

For more information email at clagrow@sbcglobal.net

Steve Lamb—Page 66, 68, 81

Steve Lamb is an outstanding golfer and an avid amateur photographer. Steve's photographic works are for his enjoyment and that of his family and friends. He has no current plans to publicly exhibit or sell his works.

Yvonne Lautenschläger (aka medea)—Page 91

Yvonne is a Hamburg, Germany based artist. She has a medical degree and has worked in Orthopedic Medicine as well as Chinese Medicine. She is married with a twenty-year-old son, a dog and two cats. She has been working as a full time painter since 2009 and is very active creating new art, writing and maintaining her blog.

To see more of Yvonne's work, visit http://www.medeasspace.de

Jackie Spector Linder—Page 89

Jackie has been a Mosaic Artist since 1999, when she decided to turn a life long passion for Mosaics into a fulltime occupation. She is recent transplant to Northern Westchester, New York where she is a member of the Katonah Museum Artists Association.

It is Jackie's belief that mosaic art is an opportunity to recycle and reuse items that would otherwise be discarded. In a puzzle-like fashion, Jackie's artistic process begins with one small piece of stained glass, china or ceramic tile. Her portfolio includes but, is not limited to mirrors, tables, frames and clocks. Jackie can be reached either through her website **jackiespectorlinder.weebly.com** or on her facebook page Jackie Spector Linder mosaic artist.

Craig Mann—Page 57

Craig Mann recently graduated in game design & theory from London South Bank University, previously studying animation and multimedia at A levels.

He enjoys creating digital art inspired by fantasy and comic book styles, working in different types of animation and creating 3D environments to explore. He is currently working freelance as an illustrator and as a artist on a soon to be released app.

View his work and contact me at **http://www.craigmanndesigns.co.uk**, **https://www.facebook.com/pages/Craig-Mann-MultiMedia/290364926354** or at **craigmanndesigns@gmail.com**

Yalily Mejia—Page 75

Dominican mosaic artist Yalily Mejia has been working with glass for more that 14 years. She began working with stain glass in her early teens.

She is a self taught mosaic artist who likes to experiment with different styles and materials. Everything inspires; from nature, to art, to human behavior, to music, and even a fragance can lead her to explore new things. Her main material is stained glass, but stone, smalti, ceramics, wood, and all kinds of things can be used for mosaics.

View her work and contact her on facebook at
http://www.facebook.com/yalilymejiamosaics

Mongobi-Bibbiana T. Mele—Page 21, 32, 88

Mongobi-Bibbiana T. Mele was born in Sardinia and lives and works in Florence. She has a Master of Arts degree and then studied at the Faculty of History of Arts and graduated in Museology. After that she specialized in Contemporary Art. For 13 years (1999-2011) she was part of the teaching staff of the Centre for Contemporary Art Luigi Pecci in Prato. In 2000 she received the International Award "Art Literature" organized by Sergio Polillo at GAMeC of Bergamo. She has published studies and assays with Lubrina Publisher in 2002, Jaca Book Idearte in 2003 and in 2004.

She uses the collage technique because her creativity flows so fast.

She has exhibited her works in, New York, Denver, Madrid and in Italy Florence, Turin, Rome, Salerno, Rimini, Sesto San Giovanni (Milan) Naples.

Artist Web site: **http://www.mongobi.it/**

Link for my published collage **http://www.mongobi.it/works/energy/bodily-collage/bodily-collage.html**

http://www.tumblr.com/blog/bibbiana-mele-mongobi

http://www.facebook.com/pages/Mongob%C3%AC-collage/166479643503435

http://kolajmagazine.com/artistdirectory/mongobi-bibbiana-mele

MOO Monika Mori—Page 30

MOO Monika Mori was born in 1960 in Moedling (Austria) and had formal trainings by Prof. Anneliese Beschorner. Since 2008, her work has been internationally exhibited and is included in major and private collections.

MOO interpretes—as Goethe remarked—the art as a mediator of the unspeakable. She communicates through her works and wants to re-animate, in the native word-sense! Monika Mori, known as the artist MOO, works with bold colors and strokes, allowing free elements of drips and dashes to bisect her canvases. Her works are highly expressive—she has always wanted the world to hear what she has to say, and these artistic communications embody her emotions, experiences and her delight at the interaction with color. For MOO, color is liberating. Only through art can one mediate the unspeakable, so this allows for a greater freedom within a work. It is a language unto itself and there is merit to all interpretations. The subtle earth palette glows from the surface of the canvas and illuminates the striking dripped forms. Their uneven linear progress forms crowds, forests, circuitry—they travel and lead us on through the painting and beyond. The strength of these paintings reflects the strength of MOO herself, and the intensity of the message she has to convey.

Monika Mori currently lives in Austria and Florida, United States.

View her work on her website at: www.mori-art.at

Or on facebook at: https://www.facebook.com/pages/MORI-ART-MOO/10150108071750372

Vhilo Persson —Page 84

Vhilo H. Persson was born in 1972 in Sweden. He is a self taught artist. His dedication to his artwork has helped him over come many hardships in life. These include a homeless period and three bouts with cancer. In his words "My Art Saved My Life And If I Don't Paint I Die. It Is That Simple."

His work has exhibited in Sweden, United States, and Brussels. He is represented by a gallery in New York and his art will be in art fairs this year around the world. View his work at: www.vhilo-artist1.se or https://www.facebook.com/pages/Vhilo/141107109237647?ref=hl

Contact his at: www.vhilo-artist1.se

Leslie Rodreguez—Page 11, 28, 72, 87

Leslie is a mixed media artist, she creates with just about anything, and her favorite medium is acrylic paint. She uses plaster, wood, fibers and paper in her art. Leslie tends to like dark colors and neutrals, but for some reason always end up with vibrant and loud colors in her art. She just goes with the flow, and she lets her imagination fly. She is currently pursuing her Associate's Degree in graphic arts and has an etsy shop. She is the mother to 3 teenage boys and has two pit bulls and a Chihuahua.

View her work at: www.Lesliero.com and www.facebook.com/lelart

Contact her at: 812-207-1630 or lesliemro@yahoo.com

Barry Stein—Page 52

Inspired by an intense love of nature. A self-taught Oregon, artist Barry Stein spends hours in the wild researching the wildlife and their surroundings that come to life in his world-renown bronze sculptures. Currently, Barry's work can be found in prestigious collections throughout the world, and are presently on display in The Waldorf Astoria Hotel New York City, The New York Hilton Hotel, New York Essex House, Hyatt Regency, The Venetian Ho-

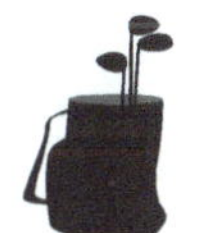

tel in Las Vegas, the Hilton Hotel in Honolulu, and galleries in many states throughout the U.S. as well as galleries in England, France and Germany. Barry's wildlife sculptures have been presented as gifts by our government's executive branch to foreign heads of state.

Rather than start his process in clay, as most bronze artists do, Barry's sculpture process begins by creating his wildlife art in wood. The relative softness of clay or wax allows for corrections, which can make the process much easier. But wood, the more difficult medium, offers the artist the option of more detail.

Once a carving is completed, the process of converting the figure into bronze begins: the making of an initial mold, then the wax casting which creates the shape of the final mold into which the molten bronze is poured, followed by the actual casting of the sculpture. Painstaking cleaning and polishing are followed by the application of the patinas that give the figure it's final beautiful coloring.

View his work at: www.barrystein.com

Contact him at barrystein@msn.com or 800 695 4388

Tony Steinhauer—Page 9, 32, 82

Tony Steinhauer is an architectural designer and a photographer based in Hattiesburg, Mississippi. With a degree in Architectural Engineering, Tony has been designing hotels, restaurants, and homes all over the southeastern United States for the last thirteen years. He is the sole owner of Hub City Designers, LLC, which specializes in custom home/business design and business logos. Originally from New Hebron, Mississippi, Tony also dabbles in wood crafts, in addition to his work in photography & art. He can be reached at tony@hubcitydesigners.com.

View his work at www.facebook.com/SteinhauerPhotography and www.facebook.com/hubcitydesigners.

Ben Thompson—Page 14, 59

Ben Thompson grew up in York. Having achieved a BA Honors First Class in Illustration and Animation at Manchester Metropolitan University, he continued studies with a Masters at the Royal College of Art, London. Throughout his studies and professional career BT has concentrated on the creation of experimental film, video, text, sound and performance, however over the past few years this focus has become directed toward composing

Collages or 'Faux-Documents' as he regards them. BT's collages are composed by hand using imagery direct from publications. View his work at: **www.BTcollage.com**

Jesse Treece—Page 90

Jesse Treece is a collage artist living in Seattle, WA whose work screams of the simple, yet ever complex, interpretations of both the mundane and whimsical facets of life. He's somehow managed to mix both the regular and absurd, beautiful and disturbing and put them into images that you find you could get lost in for hours. His tools of the trade include scissors, glue and vintage magazines/books.

View his work at: **www.collageartbyjesse.tumblr.com**
https://www.facebook.com/collageartbyjesse
Contact him at: **collageartbyjesse@yahoo.com**

Julie Wheler—Page 18, 42

Julie Wheler includes golf and one of the many sports she enjoys Photography is a favorite hobby. She enjoys photographing all aspects of nature.

Marian Williams—Page 23, 41, 55, 83

Marian Williams, born in Rotterdam, is a self-taught collage artist, living and working in France. Using only authentic photos and illustrations from vintage and modern magazines and books, she creates dynamic, striking, colorful collages.

Classical art, retro chic and kitsch are combined in a challenging way she calls 'The Art of Inferior Decoration'.

Her first collage art exhibition in France took place in April 2011, since then she has been exhibited internationally. Her works are compositions of original illustrations from books and magazines dating from 1900 till today.

The early compositions are created with exclusively paper, lately combined with both acrylic and oil paint.

View her works on facebook at **https://www.facebook.com/pages/Marian-Williams-Collage-art/161052390617048?ref=hl** on her website **http://marianwilliams.artweb.com/** at KOLAJ MAGAZINE / ARTIST DIRECTORY: **http://kolajmagazine.com/artistdirectory/marian-williams** or contact her at **itswishcraft@aol.com**

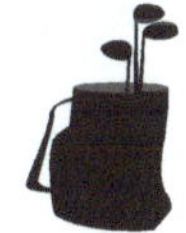

Katherine Wood—Page 15, 58, 76

Katherine Wood is a mixed media artist. You may know her as "Miz Katie" around the web. She started painting in 2008. Painting has been her childhood dream come true. She envisioned herself as an artist at a very young age. Katie likes to paint people from photographs, and she likes to make up stuff as she goes along, too. Katie has lots of characters living in her head, banging on the bars of their cage, wanting out. She also loves painting abstracts with palette knives. She lives in Kansas with her husband, two dogs, and three cats.

View her work at: blog—**http://www.mizkatie.com/**

FB—**https://www.facebook.com/mizkatie**

FB page—**https://www.facebook.com/KJWoodartist**

Purchase Katie's art—**https://www.etsy.com/shop/mizkatie**

Laurel Woolstenhulme—Page 95

Laurel has had a passion for art since she was a small child and has always had the ability to visualize things in her head and then create them with her hands. She received her BA from Southern Utah University in 1999. Over the years, she has experimented with many different art forms including making tile mosaics, painting, jewelry making, and even building competitive gingerbread houses. In 2012, she discovered her true passion of creating 3-D paper art. Her artistic process takes many hours and a steady hand, but she loves what she does and each piece of art is filled with joy and creative energy. Laurel currently lives in Washoe Valley, Nevada in the shadow of the beautiful Sierra Nevada Mountains with her husband and three children. For more information, visit her blog at **laurel-thepaperartist.blogspot.com**, her Etsy store **www.etsy.com/shop/the-paperartist**, email her at **laurel.r.wool@gmail.com** or see regular updates of her current work by liking her facebook page at "The Paper Artist (Laurel Woolstenhulme)".

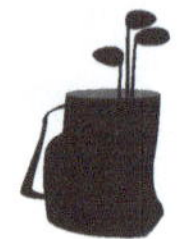

Index of Quotations

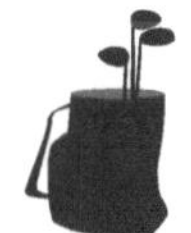

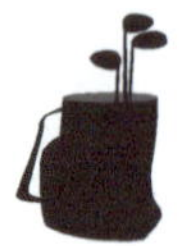

About the Author

BRADFORD G. WHELER is the former CEO, President and Co-owner of Allan Electric Company. He sold the company to a New York Stock Exchange listed company back when the stock market was hot. After staying on as President during the transition period, Brad retired.

Brad's lifelong love of history, art, books and the inherent humor in man's nature lead to the founding of BookCollaborative.com. and the publishing of this book as well as "CAT SAYINGS wit & wisdom from the whiskered ones" "HORSE SAYINGS: wit & wisdom straight from the horse's mouth", DOG SAYINGS: wit & wisdom from man's best friend", and "SNAPPY SAYINGS; wit & wisdom from the world's greatest minds".

Brad's various community involvements include being a Trustee of Community General Hospital in Hamilton, NY and Chairing their Finance Committee. He is the former Chairman of the Board of Trustees of Cazenovia College, Former Chairman and member of the Board of Directors and Alumni Association and President of the Sigma Phi Society at Cornell University in Ithaca, NY. He is also a former member of the Board of Directors of the Greater Cazenovia Area Chamber of Commerce and several other boards.

Brad played polo on Cornell University's men's polo team for four years and was a member of the Cazenovia Polo Club. In 2011 he was inducted into the Manlius Pebble Hill Athletic Hall of Fame.

Brad holds a BS and ME in Civil and Environmental Engineering from Cornell University in Ithaca, NY as well as an MBA degree from Fordham University in New York, NY.

Brad, his wife Julie, and their Golden Retriever Quincy live in Cazenovia, NY.

www.ingramcontent.com/pod-product-compliance
Lightning Source LLC
LaVergne TN
LVHW052254100826
845147LV00001B/39

* 9 7 8 0 9 8 2 2 5 3 8 5 4 *